Tropic Days

Part II The Passing Face

by

E. J. Banfield

Double9 BOOKS

Tropic Days

Part II The Passing Face

by E. J. Banfield

ISBN: 978-93-69071-62-3

Published by

DOUBLE 9 BOOKS

2/13-B, Ansari Road
Daryaganj, New Delhi – 110002
info@double9books.com
www.double9books.com
Tel. 011-40042856

ABOUT THE AUTHOR

Edmund James Banfield was an English-born author and naturalist who became well-known for his works about the tropical life of Queensland, Australia. Born on September 4, 1852, in Liverpool, United Kingdom, Banfield moved to Australia, where he spent much of his life on Dunk Island, off the coast of Queensland. His deep connection to the island and its environment informed much of his writing, which often explored the flora, fauna, and the everyday life of the region. Banfield is best remembered for his 1908 book Confessions of a Beachcomber, in which he reflects on his experiences living in isolation on Dunk Island. He also authored Tropic Days (1918), a series of personal observations on the tropical world, and Last Leaves from Dunk Island. His intimate, detailed descriptions of the natural world and his exploration of the relationship between people and their surroundings garnered recognition as a significant contribution to Australian literature. Banfield's grave on Dunk Island is listed on the Queensland Heritage Register, marking his lasting legacy in the region. He passed away on June 2, 1923, at the age of 70, leaving behind a unique body of work focused on the tropical landscapes he loved.

CONTENTS

THE CORROBOREE 7

THE CANOE-MAKER 11

TWO LADIES 16

SOOSIE 22

BLUE SHIRT 36

THE FORGOTTEN DEAD 39

EAGLES-NEST FLOAT 42

NATURE IN RETALIATION 44

"STAR RUN ABOUT" 47

BLACKS AS FISHERMEN 50

THE CORROBOREE

"No ceremony that to great ones 'longs."

SHAKESPEARE.

Summoned, invited, children, men, women, and piccaninnies assembled to participate in the duties and recreations of the moment.

Message-sticks had been carried into unfamiliar country by nervous boys. One of the organisers at ease with his pen sent to his kin formal and official invitations mingled with social and affectionate greetings. All responded.

The beach sent its silent-footed contingents trailing along the yellow sands, carrying in well-worn dilly-bags oysters and scraps of half-baked fish smeared with smoke, and gritty. All their lives had they trudged along the convenient margin of the sea, where the receding tide leaves a firm, level, springy track. They were familiar with all its moods, and took little heed of any.

The fame of a previous Parliament had spread far and wide, even to that aspect of the Dividing Range which sends its waters to the great shallow gulf to the west. Natives who, though living among the mountains but two days' journey from the coast, had never seen the sea, hastened thither in bee-line, passing through unknown but not unfriendly country. Though the age of tribal feuds was past, special weapons of defence were carried, for did not strange jungles teem with spectral denizens whom imagination endowed with appalling shape, with cunning, and with rending ferocity? Unmolested, the party arrived one evening, to gaze with mute astonishment on the sea. It was almost as incomprehensible, and therefore almost as fearsome, as the phantoms of the bush. Mysterious, vast beyond the range of vision, here grumbling on the sand, there mingling with the sky, the strangers peered at it through the screen of whimpering casuarinas and trembled. The rustle of the subsiding north-easter made for fear. They told one another that the big salt water was alive. It talked in austere tones, while their own sleepy lagoons were silent and tame. Wonderingly, they retreated to the jungle for the night, there to take counsel of the long-shoremen.

"That b-i-g fella salt water, him talk all asame?"

"Yowi! Him sing out plenty. Mak'm b-i-g fella row!"

"That fella him walk about lika that?"

"Yowi! Him walk about. Quiet little bit. Sometime run about splash'm water; mak'm boat capsize. Plenty men drown finis!"

The strangers shivered and longed to return to their cool hills; but the long-shoremen beguiled them with descriptions of the fish and the crabs and oysters the generous sea gave, and told that in the morning it would be "quiet fella" and that they need not be afraid.

With taut-strung nerves, the highlanders approached the sea, which shone in matutinal placidity. When the ripples wavered on the smooth sand and ran in caressing ripples towards their feet, they started and shrunk. The incomprehensible ocean was alive and much to be feared, for was it not so big that no one could see where it ended? They sat and watched its enticing gestures, and, gathering courage, stood tremulously while the tide splashed their feet and retreated. The boldest walked in ankle-deep and danced in daredevilry, and soon young and old were gambolling uncouthly, tasting the sea's quality, shouting and splashing. None ventured more than knee-deep; some crawled and wallowed in the wet sand, too fearful to trust their lives to so big a thing which showed itself to be alive by breathing and moving. The morning was spent in moist frolics, and when the north-easter began to work up a little sea, which spoke in menacing tones, the terrified strangers withdrew.

Late in the afternoon the corroboree began, many of the participators having spent hours in the assumption of the festive costume of the down of sulphur-crested cockatoos plastered to the skin with grease and the blood. It is not to be supposed that white down in the hands of experienced dressers is incapable of variation in style. Several original designs excited the approbation of spectators. The down was arranged in tufts following the perpendiculars of the body from shoulder to shin, or in a series of circles accurately spaced, or in intersecting spirals, while the heads of all performers and combatants were converted into white mops.

And with the clapping of hollowed hands and the clicking of boomerangs the function began. And having danced to their own satisfaction and the delight of the crowd, the warriors with ostentation and bluster recited private grievances and challenged those against whom they had real or fancied wrongs to combat. Most of the noisy declamation was ill-founded. The many had no grievances and no intentions of fighting, but out of the shouting crowd stepped two big men who sought compensation for "another Helen." Though not lovely or winsome or an heiress, she sufficed as the motive for an honourable and public strife, quite as sincere as many of the scuffles without the walls of Troy. Spears and boomerangs were thrown viciously and dodged and evaded skilfully until one of the men found a boomerang sticking fast in his leg. The wound was decisive, and with much hullabaloo the defeated warrior limped away, while the lady, whom niggardly Nature had denied the grace of blushing, passively went to the victor.

Among the strangers to the coast was an old man but a yard and a quarter high, with unkempt, grisly beard, a head which needed not the glorification of cockatoo's down, long, thin arms, huge hands, thick, stump legs, and sprawling feet. No far-reaching crab of the reef just showing its worn brown tusks off-shore was more grotesque of mien and gait. To emphasise his malignant mood, he carried a huge boomerang, which seemed to obey and embody his whims. It sprang from his powerful hands in resolute and impetuous flight, whirred threateningly overhead, and returned to foot, fluttering and purring, as if endowed with affection for its unlovable master. None so mastered the missile; but for all his weird influence over it, he was subject to the restraints of another weapon which seldom left his hands. Is there not a spiritual law which imposes checks on the bombastic tricks of crude and cultured alike, or was it by force of gravity that the point of the dwarf's long and slender spear dipped into the ground, punctuating mock martial struts with perverse irregularity? Prodigious in his own estimation, his jibes and taunts were almost as terrifying as the erratic flights of his boomerang; for the dwarf was a privileged individual, the Thersites of the campaign, and with one advantage over his prototype—he really wanted to fight. So he swaggered, heeding not the reproving spear; he fumed; he mocked; for no warrior affected to notice his vainglorious absurdities. He was as much in earnest as those who fought on account of elemental love, and far more so than any of the blusterers who talked big and looked small. He longed to fight, and for money.

Each warrior was challenged individually, and when none responded he railed against all for cowards and sent the boomerang hissing defiance against the blue sky, to fall with mutter and thud at his feet. In his rage the little man became hysterical, and the more he scolded the less important, while the swaying spear emphasised increasing agitation, but brought him neither humility nor jibe, for the race does not intentionally relieve its drama with comedy.

No more influential personage was present than "Mooty," the crafty, determined, plausible philosopher—the sagest of the counsellors, the most flowery of orators, the most weird of the wizards. Long before he had established his reputation as a medicine-man. A settler had purchased some cast-off goats in a distant town, and had employed a black boy of the district as assistant drover, and the name of the boy was Tom. Since there are many "Toms," a distinguishing surname had to be bestowed, so "Goat" was affixed, and as "Tom Goat" the stranger was known. Having no sweetheart, he made love to several dusky dames, all of whom rejected him because his absurd name made him a figure for fun. Rosey, wife of Jack, was persistently courted, and scornfully she despised her wooer. That individual, however, was not without malignant resource. Rosey complained of a sore throat, and as she got worse her boy became similarly afflicted. The faces and throats of both swelled alarmingly, so that Mooty, who had the cases in hand, gave up hope. Both were resigned, when Mooty, to his own horror and the dismay of everyone, caught the dread disease.

No such illness had ever been known in the district, and since it had not only baffled Mooty's skill, but had irreverently seized him—the only physician of credit and renown—its cause must be supernatural. Thus did he reason, as he began occult investigations. Jack and Rosey lay in their camp passively dying. Mooty prowled about, the sleeves of a discarded shirt tied under his distended jaws. No physical origin for the mysterious disease was found during the two days he devoted to methodic search and secret rite. Then an anticipated discovery rewarded him and made his name thrill among his race. To a condescending white man he told of his skill in these terms:

"Two fella him close up finis. Me bin look out camp belonga two fella. B'mbi me bin find'm little fella fork stick close up alonga groun'. Me frait. My word, me bin pick'm up easy fella. Me look out longa little fella hole. Me bin see hair, too much, belonga Tom Goat. That hair bin mak'm two fella no good. Him mak'm me fella no good. Me catch'm that fella hair along two fella stick. Tchuck'm along ribber. My word! That fella hair no good! Him go phuff! Kill'm fish, too many. B'mbi me fella go alonga camp. Me tell'm two fella, 'You no more mak'm die. Me bin find'm that fella hair belonga Tom Goat.' B'mbi two fella him get up; him no more die; he walk about."

Exasperated by such impropriety, aghast at the consequences, Mooty—doctor alike of laws, of science, and of medicine, and a man of imperative mood—sharpened his tomahawk at the Chinaman's grindstone, theatrically testing its edge with distorted thumb. Tom Goat disappeared as silently as last night's dew, for Mooty does not hesitate to summarily administer his own judgment when his professions are scorned, his family bewitched, his countenance distorted with mumps.

With feasting and fighting, with dancing and storytelling, quarrelling and reconciliations, the assemblage spent a happy week. Then the jungle reabsorbed the nervous hillmen, and beach-combers straggled along the yellow sands.

THE CANOE-MAKER

"Last scene of all, . . . Is second childishness and mere oblivion."

SHAKESPEARE.

A tottering old man, frail alike in frame and mind, squats dying in an alien camp. His teeth have almost disappeared, worn to the gums by the mastication of food in which sand has been mingled in immoderate proportion. All his life has been spent on the verge of the sea. He has never known smooth food. Before he left his mother's breast grit was on his lips, for in her sleep she snoodled naked in the sand. Hers was the age of bark rugs or none, and was ever lord of the beach who shared with his lady so rare a comfort?

Counterparts of Cassowary's babyhood are extant to this day—milk-bellied, nose-neglected, fumbling-fingered toddlers, who smash with stones almost beyond their strength infant oysters and gulp a mixture of squash and sand.

As he grew up his food, seared on a fire on the beach, was always more or less gritty. Possibly it would hardly have been relished if the accustomed condiment had been absent.

For many a long year Cassowary was a sort of king in the locality of his birth, though this rank brought him no isolation. Now he is without rank and grim in his lonesomeness. True to the sentiments of his race, the men and women who knew him when he was strong and lusty strive to make him comfortable in his dotage; but he is repellent. His surliness does not vex them. They pity and excuse and endeavour to soothe. To strangers whom Cassowary has never loved and would now assault with spear and nulla-nulla, they apologise.

"Poor fella, Cassowary. Him no good. Close up that fella finis."

Then they tell of his strange fantasies. Similar delusions have afflicted notable men of the world, and even to this day are there not apprehensive monarchs whose precautions are similar to those of the age-worn savage?

He imagines that he is regarded as a useless encumbrance, and that his fellows would gladly hasten his departure to that country on the bourne of which he painfully lingers. Suspicious of plots to rob him of the poor vestiges of life, he is ever on his guard against poison, his special dread. Rather than run risk he submits to semi-starvation, for the decayed monarch of a narrow strip of shore has no servitor on whom to impose the office of taster of his dishes. A stranger may of his goodwill offer a tribute of tobacco. It is cast away with every manifestation of indignation and haste. He is sure that the one solace of existence has been drugged, and that if he indulges he must die. How marvellous the self-denial! How many of us would purchase half an hour's existence such as his at the cost of declining the one luxury of life!

Flour from his master's hands is served like the stranger's tobacco, though he may not have tasted food for days; nor does he accept a portion of the damper cooked in his presence until he has seen others eat. Then he feeds reluctantly and with extreme caution, not to gratify the palate, but to maintain life.

Was ever monarch or Roman pontiff beset by more vindictive and envious foes than this helpless old savage who possesses nothing save a grimy shirt and the fragments of a blanket?

Cassowary, an old man when I first met him, was of the sort which does not make friends with white men. Silent, resolute, reserved, a man apart, he disdained the race-shattering language his fellows hastened to acquire. His pidgin English, limited to a few words, was almost as unintelligible as his own rude tongue. Once I landed on the beach which was his favourite resort, and as the anchor slipped into the sea, smoke puffed and drifted from the camp and the lonesome man's dogs barked; but by the time the camp was reached the smell of the fire had gone, and all tracks had been obliterated as if by the efficient touch of the wind. The heat of the sand at the entrance of the dome-shaped humpy revealed the site of the covered embers, and the rest was silence.

At the back of the humpy, concealed by carelessly disposed bark and grass, was a bark canoe which Cassowary, fisherman and oyster-eater, was never without. In those days he deserved the reputation of being an unrivalled maker of canoes which, during the first few weeks of their prime, were sound, neat of appearance, quite seaworthy, though of small dimensions and exceedingly light. Others might be expert fishermen and skilful in more exacting sport of turtle and dugong catching, but all acknowledged his special superiority. Though custom had made him a king, Nature had designed him for a canoe-maker, while with that invincible irony with which she rebukes the self-esteem and baffles the ambitions of mortals, she discounted her gift by the bestowal of frank distrust of the sea. He was so impelled to the exercise of the one talent that during youth and manhood his chief occupation and never-ending delight lay therein. That which his right hand had found to do he did with all his might, his frail craft being the admiration of all, while the confidence with which others managed them proved their quality. They toyed with the sea in its placid moods, and were deferential in its ill-humour. But Cassowary never ventured beyond easy hail from the shore, however urgent the occasion or propitious the day.

Fear also restricted his wanderings in the bush, which kept him within sound of the dreaded waves. He was an unaffected beach-comber. Neither the food-bestowing sea nor the safe dry land was for him.

By instinct he seemed to be guided to the best trees for bark, generally selecting "gulgong," though others were equally pliant in his hands. Raw from the tree, he would soak the single sheet in water, and while sodden steam it over a smoky fire, and, as it softened, mould it with hand and knee. Bringing the edges of the end designed for the stem into apposition, using a device on the principle of the harness-maker's clamp, he sewed them together with strips of freshly cut cane. Two stretchers gave to the craft beam, and the necessary sheer and thwart-ship stays of twisted cane stiffness. Gunwales of cane were sewn on, the stitches being cemented with gum made plastic by frequent renderings over the fire on a flat stone, and then the canoe was complete save for the hand-paddles, spoon-bowl-shaped pieces of bark.

Each canoe sat well down by the stern when the fisherman knelt in it, crouching forward like a jockey on the withers of his mount, and sending it along by the alternate strokes.

Cassowary was wont to scan each new work with the tilted head of an artist. All the stitches were regularly spaced, and since they were burnished with smoke, the canoe became a study in brown, braided with gold, representative of something more than a means towards earning a diet of fish, and inevitable grit. It was neat and of harmonious colouring; innocent of the least touch of finery; not a scratch expended on ornament. All its lines, save those of the stretchers and stays which stood for rigidity, were fluent. It was not made to model or measurement, but developed under the maker's hard hands and tough fingers—a tribute to his artistry and skill. On the water it was as blithe as a bubble.

Often had the wish to possess one of Cassowary's masterpieces arisen. He scorned barter by abandoning his property whenever the interferer appeared. When the camp was deserted while the boat was being brought to anchor there was a strong temptation to take the canoe, leaving some adequate reward. The self-denial is almost regretted, for the old man with the thin white tuft on his chin, his shyness, his hatred of strangers, and delusions of his decrepitude, are characteristic of an age soon to be of the irrecoverable past. A canoe from such accomplished hands would have represented a complimentary record of a race deficient in the elements of history.

Several years have elapsed since Cassowary made his last canoe. He acknowledged that his fingers had lost their cunning, but the fates ordained that his ideas should blossom as his manipulatory skill withered Gradually he became feeble in mind and body, and was wont to spend his time crouched in a rough shelter dreaming prodigious dreams. He would wake not only his fellows, but a pitying neighbour of other complexion, with enthusiastic shouts announcing that a "big fella steamer" was whistling out at sea; that it was his steamer; that it carried two bags of flour, and tea and sugar and tobacco, and one "good fella trousis"; and he would demand help in the landing of his merchandise. Worn with age, sleep would soon again claim him, but never and anon his great cry, hailing the phantom steamer with her beneficent cargo, would wake the poor and squalid camp.

The time came when Cassowary could no longer obtain for himself the coarse and trivial food essential to life, and he and another outcast, blind and maimed, quartered themselves on the camp on the beach; arid in spite of fretfulnesses and suspicions, their fellows administered to their wants. Being brought face to face with facts, the State gave orders which meant an old-age pension for the outcasts. The dole was liberal enough. The mistake was that it came too late.

There was no reaction, as is oft the case with those who retire after the bustling phase to live on the bounty of the State, for Cassowary and his blind companion had never been strenuous workers or brain-compelling men. The pension represented unexampled abundance. It was real, and yet it came from a source almost as intangible as Cassowary's ship. Food and tobacco! What more could the heart of a casual relic of such a race want? Actually he wanted nothing more, save, peradventure, a blanket; but he dreamt he did, and no earthly agent could diminish the festal extravagance of the scenes among which he revelled, conducted by the enchanted sleep.

Cassowary had at last come to his kingdom. His time had always been his own. The ready-to-hand food gave him leisure. His days were all dreams. Weary of crouching over the fire before the opening of his humpy, he began to wander in the flesh as he was wont to wander in mind. He was seen a mile away from the cheerless camp, where his companions, with smoke-dried eyes, lamented his absence.

Was he searching for a tree which might provide bark for yet another canoe—his last work, a paragon? A few days passed and it became known that Cassowary was missing. His shrunken body disordered a patch of buff sand just above high water.

Had the desolate old man, in his fancy, made the best of all canoes, and for once ventured out to sea?

TWO LADIES

"To one, resolution; to another, a disposition to dance."

NELLY, THE SHREW

As the steamer from the South enters the bay, the traveller sees ahead the fringe of houses on the low lands fronting the inlet where shipping finds safe and convenient harbourage. To the left he may be introduced to a strip of open beach between two low points of grey granite, back from which are scattered groups of modest buildings and huts which form the aboriginal settlement. The choice of the site for the settlement was influenced by the character of the country. Although but a short distance by sea from the port, it is isolated by its background of hard and inhospitable hills patched with almost impenetrable jungle. Few consigned there ever leave of their own motive, however earnest the longing may be. The home-sick realise that escape is difficult and, if successful, futile, for are not the police everywhere, and strong and compelling? Why undertake the unknown perils of unknown hills—spiritual perils more to be dreaded than physical—when capture and again banishment are certain?

Nellie Oongle-bi, among whose matrimonial experiences was Tom, of this Isle, and who since his death has gone from bad to worse, had been found under the protection of a coloured alien, sadly degenerated and saturated with opium. For her own salvation she was transported to the settlement afar off, with its frontier of sea and background of repulsive hills. She went, being in the clutches of a superior force, tractably enough, but with none of her unconquerable love of country subdued. Nelly has nothing of an attractive nature. She has a vixenish temper at times; is always on the alert for fancied slights; is by no means cleanly, unless under duress; and does not hesitate to foment subjects of quarrel. Few among her relations and friends would mourn her exile. Even her own son, Jim, was scoffingly indifferent. She was far from being so, but played her part well, being obedient, quite tame, and ever observant.

She "sat down" at the settlement, and made friends with two or three of the women there with whom she had previously been acquainted; but while she talked with apparent resignation, she scanned the hills, especially fixing in her mind a particular gully which leads up to a ridge promising an outlook to the south, upon which her hopes were fixed. Soon after dark on the second night she took to the bush, carrying a dilly-bag and a blanket. She is now one of the population of a far-distant settlement, the site of which happens to be within her own country. How she overcame the distance without food, friends, or resources, has to be told, though not altogether in her own language, for such would be unintelligible to the ordinary reader.

She was determined to run away as soon as the steamer landed her, for that part of the North was not her country, and she could not live anywhere else. Besides, she was "sorry belonga that boy Jim." During the first night of her homeward pilgrimage she never ceased walking among rocks and through the scrub, for she was fearful of being recaptured. Without pause she clambered on until well into the next day, when she slept for a little while. Then on again until dark. One big "mung-um" (mountain) stood in the hopeful direction. Thitherwards she hastened, losing count of the days and nights. Nelly has no conception of figures beyond one, two, and a great many. The climbing of the mountain occupied many days. She was bewildered, for she could not "catch'm that sal'water" which would lead her home. At last from a spur of the mountain she saw the sea—"L-o-n-g way. Too far. Me close up sing out." Though she might cry, the sight of big salt water beside which all her life had been spent was a joy and a stimulant. Pushing and worming her way through the jungle, she encountered nothing but birds, wallabies, and snakes.

Once she was startled by what seemed to be a worn narrow track. Advancing cautiously along it, she came across a huge carpet snake coiled "all a same rope alonga boat." It was asleep where an opening in the roof of vegetation made a patch of sunlight on the jungle floor, and she passed by, treading noiselessly. For food she had the fruits of the jungle, crude, harsh, and bitter. Food, indeed, was almost repugnant, for her thoughts were concentrated on her country, so she hastened down towards the now hidden sea. Far inland she heard its welcome noise—a greeting and a call from home which made her forgetful of all weariness and fret.

In course of time—a weak woman carrying a blanket and living on innutritious foods does not struggle through jungle at any remarkable speed—the foothills and then the low-lying country at the junction of two rivers were reached. Here she took off her few and bedraggled garments, and, making them into a bundle with her blanket and bag, waded through swamps, eventually emerging on a sandy beach, which she intended to follow until she regained her country, many a weary mile to the south. Providence provided an easy means of crossing the estuary of the rivers—a kindly white man, owner of a "little fella boat, little fella ingin." To him she told the story of her escape and her longing for her own country and her own people, and was ferried across. Then she picked up a camp of her race, the members of which, sympathising with her, accompanied her on her way for a couple of days. One day she woke from her sleep on the edge of the mangroves with her blanket sopping with blood which had flowed from her mouth and nose during sleep. "Me bin sorry belonga that boy Jim. Me bin sorry belonga country. That 'nother country no good belonga me. Me think me die. Me walk alonga sandy beach. Some time alonga b-i-g fella rock. Me close up tumble down altogether. Me tired. B'mbi catch'm Liberfool Crik (Liverpool Creek). Plenty fella sit down. He bin sing out, 'Hello! You come back from that place?' Me bin say 'Yes; that country no good belonga me.'"

A month or so after Nelly was again found in the service of a coloured alien, tugging away with another weak gin at what she calls a "two-fella saw." For her task of sleeper-cutting her reward would probably be a handful of rice and a dose of opium per day.

Nelly is now at her leisure within a mile or so from the place of her birth, hardly conscious of the feat represented by her solitary pilgrimage. Occasionally she has the company of her tall and indifferent boy. She enjoys the society of her relations, and indulges as oft as may be in exhilarating misunderstandings with them. Without a vehement squabble now and again life would be intolerably insipid. Anger, accompanied by fluent abuse, is to her a kind of spiritual blood-letting for the casement of her suddenly plethoric temperament. But such is of her frailty. Proof of her strength of purpose, has it not been given?

MARIA DANCES

In her youth Maria gave promise of a rare condition among coastal blacks—tendency to width and breadth. As she grew in bulk she seemed, if not to decrease in stature, at least to remain stationary. Thus it was that her figure became perfect.

If there be one feature of animal physiology more adorable than aught else in the eyes of the lords of the soil, it is fat—fat under any and every circumstance. They admire it in animals of the chase, and the paltry, greasy relics of a feast may be smeared over the body with something of the pride and gratification derivable in other and cleaner walks of life from perfumed powder, pink and white.

Being fat and shiny as a girl, Maria had keen and ardent lovers. She was an adorable novelty.

Blacks do not gaze into the faces of their sweethearts. They have never found chaste delight in the writing of woeful ballads to their mistress's eyebrows, or to the glorification of their snubby and expansive noses. If any of Maria's admirers had been lyrical, her buxom condition would have been the theme of their idealisations. In time she became the mother of children, still retaining that charming superiority of bulk which excited the rage of sisters whose skins did not shine, whose flesh did not quiver whensoever they walked, talked, or even smiled.

No marvel that her matrimonial experiences were the comment of the camp and gave rise to many differences, but, since placidity and fat have been known among so-called civilised peoples to blend in the individual, Maria's demeanour called for no comment. It was not her fault, but the flightiness and whimsicality of Nature which had contrived to make her the belle of the camp. And why not enjoy the obvious admiration of the stalwart youths as well as the discomfort of the sisters who had not an ounce of irresistible fascination of which to boast.

For some years the form of Maria had not waddled across accustomed scenes. Quite unexpectedly it loomed up as large and buoyant as ever. The light-hearted denizens of the camp had arranged an evening's entertainment. The fires burned low, the sea babbled, making white-skirted frolic on the hard level sand, and the piping voices of the honey-seeking flying foxes among the tea-trees seemed to chide the parrots of the day for having left so little refreshment in the blossoms. Behind a screen of faded blankets the warriors of the camp were adorning themselves with white clay and feathers and long, shaggy beards of bark, while the leader of the orchestra began to tune his boomerang and fire-hardened sticks, and his attendants to squat ready to drum on thighs and lap with hollowed hand in time with his refrain and clicking music. The fires flared up, and the band emerged with thumping step and emphatic grunts to illustrate the ceremonious visit of strangers to a camp at which the nature of the reception was in doubt. One individual, in chalk for the most part, advanced, half nervously, half anxiously, to the musician, and modestly retired, and advanced again and retired, until reassured, and then the crowd came forward whirling and grunting, and, with high-waving arms in unison and swaying bodies, gave token of happiness.

ACT II.—The master of ceremonies carried to the front a big and rough sapling. The fires glowed again, the orchestra clicked and thumped, and a single boy in an ancient red handkerchief and chalks danced into the light, and, keeping time with the music, began in pantomime to fashion the sapling into a sword, using a fictitious shell, with which he scraped off imaginary bark. While absorbed in his work, his companions came from the screen in haste, skipping round him and mimicking all his actions and grunting in unison with him, while making the sand-ridge to quiver with intensity of tread. Presently all flopped down on haunches in close formation round the sword-maker, still maintaining rhythmical sway of body and limb, and while some held the sapling, others toiled strenuously towards the completion of a good and true weapon, the master of ceremonies encouraging and exhorting the workers until nature could hold out no longer, and they bounded to their feet and, with grunts and signs and with bodies reeking with perspiration, whirled away into darkness.

ACT III.—Each of the noisy players came suddenly into the glare carrying a rotund, compact bundle, and, squatting down, began with grunts and sighs the great "coco-nut" act, obviously one of the masterpieces of the corroboree. In perfect time the sham coco-nuts were beaten with hands in lieu of sticks or tomahawks, while the accompaniment became faster and faster. Ever and anon each, still rocking, would peer closely at his prize to satisfy himself as to its quality, and forthwith continue the resonant belabouring of the shell, until the meat therein was available with joyous shout.

ACT IV.—Most of the accumulated bark and leaves having by this time passed into flame and smoke, the attendants raided the nearest gunyah for fresh supplies of material for illumination. The big fires lit up the arena anew, and, marshalled by the conductor, the band rushed out of the darkness uttering grunts which rang a change on the monotony of previous vocal efforts. A masterpiece of composition, it conjured up the dimness of the jungle and the smell of damp vegetation. All squatted in a double ring, back to back. This formation was not strictly maintained, for each individual made half turns to right and left alternately, simultaneously scratching the sand with distended fingers and kicking vigorously until the sand ascended in the smoke-tinged glow, heads bowing and ducking with mechanical regularity, as the entertainers sought—and with conspicuous success—to portray a community of scrub turkeys building an incubating mound.

Then it was that the favourite and belle of the camp, the fascinating creature whose magnificent condition bestowed privileges undreamt of by other ladies, became conspicuous. Her costume had evidently been designed for a lady not divinely tall, but considerably less of flesh than the wearer. Maria did not actually overflow, though perilously near that point. Surely buttons were never designed to resist such strain. Coloured ladies generally sit meekly among the audience and chatter and maintain the drum-beats, lacking which no corroboree could be successful. During the intervals they may emboss pictures in the impressionable sand with cunning forefinger and giggle, for the subjects are often quaint. Maria, sure of her privileges, waddled out from the flame-obscuring dusk, turned an ample back upon the double ring of boys, and played her part as one of the giddy and industrious wild-fowls. Her fingers scratched the air and her feet the dust with a realism not to be excelled by the most gifted of the boys, while her half grunt, half chuckle, exactly imitative of the social garrulity of the turkey, gave artistic finish to a scene which would have been absolutely delusive if feathers had been in fashion. Maria, a fleer at mere ponderosity, skipped and whisked from left to right with fay-like airiness of foot until a thrill of delight went through the camp. The frolicsome turkeys scratched and scattered leaves that were not, and gobbled and clucked, until, panting and perspiring, all rose, and with a simultaneous shout scampered for the screen, while the master of ceremonies shouted "Finis!" The music ceased, the flames faded, and substantial Maria dissolved in the gloom.

SOOSIE

"No legend! Well, let us invent one."—SCOTT.

A crinkled fist, fumbling and twisting, protruded from a rent in a dilapidated dilly-bag. It had done so with infinite feebleness for many an hour in unavailing protest against the woes and weight of life, for faint scratch smeared with blood denoted the friction of tender skin against the broken edges of the cane-made bag.

A scarcely audible, inhuman wail—pathetically staccato—told of unceasing pain. Whomsoever the bag contained was enduring martyrdom.

"That fella, him no good. Close up finis. B'mbi me plant'm along scrub."

Thus spoke the pleasant-faced gin who passed with the dilly-bag along a narrow aisle of the jungle, intent upon ridding herself of a vexatious encumbrance, and at the same time performing the rite of unrighteous burial.

Squirming in dirt was a naked infant-black, foul, and but a few days old.

"Mother belonga that fella him dead—finis. That fella, him no good. Him sing out all a time. More better tchuck'm away."

Frail outcast—the very scum of a blacks' camp, its repulsiveness was tragic. Dirt and odour sickened, yet its appeal was irresistible. That universal language, a human cry, which everywhere and always quickened the pulse, stirred pity to its depths. I seized the stained bag (it was a desperate deed) and, breaking down its worn sides, displayed its contents—a girl in all the infamy of neglect, starvation, and dirt—a panting mummy reeking with offence.

Spreading out a handkerchief, I put the awful atom on it gingerly, while the foster-mother reiterated her counsel to "tchuck'm alonga scrub."

In the guise of a frail bundle at arm's-length was Soosie conducted to a civilised home.

Dismay tempered with pity greeted her.

"How horrible! How dirty!"

"Is it really a little girl? It looks like a wild animal."

"Do let me nurse it."

Thus was crinkled-faced Soosie welcomed.

Many successive baths did she endure, faintly wailing, until dirt soaked off and the wails ceased for the time being as Soosie sucked ravenously at a tiny sugar-bag.

What a frail little life it was—feeble beyond expression, and ugly with the ugliness of savagery. She wriggled and screwed up her skinny features with inane ferocity. A motherless wallaby would have submitted to human solace and ministrations with daintier mien; but the whole household thrilled with excitement. Could the spluttering spark of life be made to glow? That was the all-absorbing topic for days. Gradually some sort of a human rotundity became manifest, and on the occasion of the bath it was more and more apparent that instead of being impenetrably black the skin-tint was a mingling of pale brown and pink; and as regular nourishment began to be effective the features changed, losing their gross animalism.

Just because of the waif's helplessness was repugnance to her conquered. She had no other redeeming quality. In a certain sense she was fearsome; she required unremitting attention and care; her whimpering fits, in beast-like monotone, shook the nerve of the most patient of her attendants. She was a charge to keep and foster, and the duty was performed with devotion, which took little concern for self-sacrifice. Before many months had passed Soosie had been transformed into a fat roly-poly with a perpetual smile and gurgles of satisfaction, which even vocalised sleep.

All this happened years ago. In infancy Soosie had been informally adopted. She was now a bright, sensible, slender girl, whose full, melting eyes pleaded for inevitable facial defects, and whose complexion was very greatly at fault. She grew up more averse from the manners and moods of her mother than those of us who better understand the differences of race. To her a black was more abhorrent than a snake. She loathed the sight of those who came about the place, and would not defile herself by touching the cleanest—kind-hearted "Wethera," who had so nearly interred her, and to whom she was as a princess; "Wethera," who was wont to say, "That fella Tchoosie, too flash. Close up me bin tchuck'm away. Boss he bin catch'm."

Soosie evaded all possible reference to her kin, and when others spoke in sympathetic terms would say: "How can you bear to think of those horrible people who live in dirt and only half dressed in the bush? I love the scrub, and but for them would like to wander in it all day. I dare not while they are about, for some day one of them might touch me, and I would never feel clean again."

We often wondered at the irreconcilable attitude which Soosie (she was always "Miss Soosie" to all but members of the household) adopted to her own race, for she well understood where she had been born and the manner of her salvation from imminent death.

Though no special training had been hers, none of the domestic arts were unknown to her. She acquired them with ease and practised them with the air of a dignified princess and neat-handed facility. While the other children of the house stewed over lessons and rebelled against essential tasks, to Soosie everything seemed to make for holiday. She read voraciously, so that her application of English became so keen that she was the first to detect verbal dissonances. She, the youngest of two girls and a boy, would often correct their speech, not as a budding pedant, but because her ears were delicately attuned to the music of the tongue and could not, without offence, hearken to discords. She was an affected prude. Her self-chosen style of dress, her pose, her disdainful airs, her repugnance to coarse work, her inclination towards occupations and pastimes which involved isolation, showed that self-consciousness ruled her life. She lived within herself, and her life was gentle, contrasting with the boisterous playfulness of her foster sisters and brother, upon whose romps she smiled indulgently, but in which she never took part. In her own estimation she was a girl quite out of the ordinary, and one to whom the most honoured of guests must be polite, if not deferential. She exacted little niceties of demeanour from all, her equals and inferiors, for was she not treated as a daughter of the house? Often, however, in her preoccupied moods would she assume an air of detachment and jealousy towards the other children, for she could not but contrast herself with them. They were white; she was pronouncedly of the despised race. How wistfully would she scan the face of strangers! How teeming with resentment against fate her inevitable conclusions! In all save features she was white. Over her inheritance, the cruellest which fortune could bestow, she was shudderingly horrified. Not all the longings of an untainted mind could make her skin less tawny. Its stain was too deep to be blanched by the most fervent of prayers. Her outlook on life, her intensest wishes, were those of a white girl of more than decent perceptions—of actual refinement, for they tended to the avoidance of everything unpleasant and unsightly. In other respects, too, she was an absolute variant from the type, for her sensitiveness to the pain of others and of the lower animals amounted almost to a mania; for though she had a girlish horror of blood, her eagerness to solace sufferings made her so courageous that she became most apt and prompt in the administration of first aid. Her big, startled eyes showed the sincerity of her feelings, while her firm, slender fingers deftly applied bandages as she spoke in soothing tones.

The soul of a white damsel was in habitation of the body of one whose parents had been black and utterly degraded. In the days of old evil spirits were believed to be capable of taking spiteful possession of the bodies of the weak to work, in unseemlinesses and indecencies, for the mischief of the soul. Here was a good and gentle spirit which strove undemonstratively for the salvation of a being the circumstances of whose birth bordered on the infernal. It was as if the baths of infancy had purified the soul, while the permanence and perversity of blood triumphed in feature and complexion.

While the other children of the house deserved and obtained love and affection in full measure, towards Soosie were exhibited similar sentiments, with, perhaps, more consideration, for was it not plain that her life was a continual conflict—a conflict between body and soul—a body self-abhorred, a soul which needed no purification?

A creek which had its source in a ravine of the huge mountain which intercepted the rising sun and caused accustomed shadow an hour after the illumination of the western hills, ran past the lonely little house, which stood in a clearing the upright walls of which were on the sky-line scalloped with fan-palms. For many years Soosie never ventured into the jungle unaccompanied, yet she seemed to possess a sense of happenings beyond the almost solid screen of vegetation. Primal instinct contended against her affections and her love for a sheltered, clean life. Though she had always avoided association with the children of the camp, and her knowledge by imitation or precept was negative, yet was the bush an open book to her. She knew when and where to look for birds'-nests. She knew at a glance a venomous from a non-venomous snake, an edible from an inedible nut. As a child her favourite head-dress was a squat, fat mantis, the bright orange and yellow of which contrasted boldly with her fuzzy, coarse hair; and when the insect palled as an ornament it would be frizzled and slyly eaten.

Once as we strolled on the bank of the creek gazing at the lazy, red-finned fish among the swaying weeds, her wandering eyes detected a neat circular bore in the trunk of a huge silky oak. Having shrewdly scrutinised the bark, she judged the tenant to be at home. With a portion of one of the "feelers" of creeping palm stripped of all the prickles save two, she probed the tunnel and, screwing the instrument triumphantly, withdrew a huge white grub, which she ate forthwith; and then, with a grimace, assumed an air of shame and contrition, for she had astonished herself as well as others by an exhibition of untaught bush-craft and ancestral appetite.

She more than once confessed in shamefaced terms to an almost uncontrollable impulse to rush away to the mountain, that she might solace herself with the solitude and food in plenty there; but that when she conjured up the chance of meeting some "dreadful native" she thanked God for home and loving companions. How frequent and how intense was this unconfessed lust for the bush we knew not.

When Soosie was fourteen there came to the neighbourhood a hardy young fellow who began to clear a small area of jungle land; for civilisation, which had been marking time for nigh upon two decades, now marched slowly, and to no throb of drum, in our direction. Times were changing, and in some details less desirable conditions arose. The infinite privacy of the bush suffered. The little clearing was no longer our own. Soosie's demeanour became more reposeful. She had seemed to think that it might be her fate, in common with others, to become a ward of the State at some mission-station; but as settlement advanced, though still miles away, for we were the furthest out, and no interfering guardian of the peace came to enforce officialdom and insist upon obedience to the letter of the law, it was comforting to reflect that this unofficial daughter might be permitted to live out her life unhampered even by the goodwill expressed, in the first stages, by the visit of a policeman.

Her presence was necessary, not only on account of her amiable disposition and self-sacrificing ways, but for the actual load she bore of the duties of a quiet home. We had failed, however, to take into calculation the chances of another means of separation. There was now no disguising the fact that our new neighbour, Dan, was casting sheep's eyes in Soosie's direction, and to her evident dismay. It was of little avail to upbraid him as to the unseemliness of attachment to a girl who, however civilised, was of inferior race and despised colour. He frankly confessed that he wanted a wife as a companion and helpmeet; that he could not hope, in consideration of his own lowly birth and slender means and uphill task, to induce a white girl to halve his loneliness. He had studied Soosie, and was sure that she was his superior except in matter of colour. She was far better schooled and had been used to softer life.

"What," he asked, "don't you and the Missis and Miss Clare and Fan, and Bob, here, love her? You couldn't help it; and you are not ashamed. You treat her as your own child. It would be no sin for me to take her as my own wife. If she'll have me I'll marry her before the best parson in the North. What of her complexion? It's only a little more sunburnt than mine."

But Soosie was shy—more than shy. Her sensitiveness amounted to physical repulsion. She declared that, though she liked Dan, she would never marry.

"I do feel in my heart that I am nothing more than a black girl, and almost a savage. What if some day the horrible part of me got stronger, and I did go to the mountain by myself? I have heard you say that blood will tell. Often I am frightened of myself, especially when the nights are very still and I listen to the scrub hens chuckling and the flying foxes squealing, and smell the scents of the scrub. It must be very nice to live away from everybody in the very loneliest part of the big mountain, and to feel at home with actually wild things."

There was no affectation between us, so I said in comfort: "But my dear girl, you are whiter at heart than many a girl born white. It is only your skin that is dark. Perhaps if in a year or so you did marry Dan it would be the best, for a good woman, no matter what her complexion, will always earn respect. Society may not want you, but you would not want society; and it will be very many years before society hampers life in this part of the bush."

Soosie thought for a few minutes, and then replied with delicate discretion. "I can never marry Dan. Sooner or later he would despise me. It might be all right while I was young, but—we—we—blacks get old very soon. Fancy Dan having an old gin in his house; for he won't be living in a one-roomed hut all his life!"

"You are spiteful against yourself, and that's not like you, Soosie."

"I have my feelings. How else may I restrain them?" she petulantly exclaimed. "He must never think of me. It might drive me to the mountain—just to save him from me."

Dan, good fellow, was discreet. He decided to play the laggard in love, realising that any show of impetuosity might frighten Soosie. It came to be understood that in time she might see the wisdom of accepting him, and I, knowing both, and to whom mixed marriages are abhorrent, was convinced that no girl could have been better qualified to fill the position of a bushman's wife. Modest, clever, sympathetic, healthful, none of the stains of the town had ever tarnished her mind. Her voice was that of a well-schooled white girl, and all her perceptions coincided. If the wander lust was to be suppressed for ever, it seemed to me that Soosie must marry, and marry young.

While Soosie's demeanour was still the cause of earnest solicitude, a perplexing complication arose. An old man of the camp whence she had been discarded began to do his best to attract her attention.

Gifts of birds'-nests, eggs, ferns, orchids in flower, a cassowary chick, neat dilly-bags, gay with crude Pigments, were brought to the house with messages such as this:

"That fella 'Pad-oo-byer' he bin gib'em alonga 'Ky-ee-rah.'"

"Ky-ee-rah" (the evening star) had been proclaimed to be Soosie's totemic name, and "Pad-oo-byer" we knew as "Duckbill," because of a fancied resemblance to a platypus.

The gifts were tearfully repudiated. They seemed to announce that Soosie, was regarded by her mother's kin as one of themselves, notwithstanding her civilised environment.

Though for the girl's sake, not on account of any personal repugnance or despiteful attitude, the blacks had been kept at arm's length, I was on good terms with all in the district, and took interest in their doings and folk-lore. One of their primary beliefs was that children, black and white, were actually the produce of the locality, belonging, not to chance parents, but to the very land on which they were born. The germs of life, they assumed, came from the soil; the soil assimilated all flesh after death. Infants were but phases of the life with which the soil teemed. All the neighbourhood belonged to the camp—the land and everything which sprang from it, for they were the original possessors. It was their country. They argued that such things as sweet potatoes, pumpkins and mangoes, the very roses which adorned a sprawling bush, the richly tinted crotons, the flaunting alamanda over the gateway, were, strictly speaking, common property. So, too, over those children born on the place certain proprietary rights were claimed. They were akin to them, alien to their parents. Whites and blacks born in the same district must, according to their ideas, be more closely related than folks whose birthplaces were separated by distances beyond comprehension.

Such being the general opinion, fortified by undeviating oral tradition, in Soosie's case the theory was ever so much the more arguable. She was claimed, not alone on the grounds that she was a native of their own land, but because, having been born in their own camp, she must be subject to it.

Duckbill intercepted me on the edge of the clearing one morning especially to propound the law of the land.

Soosie, he told in his pidgin English, had been given to him by her uncle. She was to be his gin now that she was grown up. "More better you hunt that fella. Him want sit down alonga camp."

The bald proposition shook me, for I could not but see the logic of it from Duckbill's standpoint. He was the "big man," a wizard—ugly, old, and villainously dirty. Here was the camp's husband for the coloured girl with the white heart. The idea was revolting, and then and there I resolved at whatever cost to save the girl from such degradation.

"Clear out!" I shouted, assuming frantic anger. "You fella chuck'm Soosie away when she little fella piccaninny. That one belonga me now. Suppose you fella kick'm up row big fella government come clear you fella out. No more let you sit down longa this country."

"Country belonga me. You no humbug. You bin catch'm that fella Tchoosie l-o-n-g time. You bin make'm good fella. Belonga me now."

The disgusting old fellow went on to explain that he intended to come up to the house that evening. "You hunt'm that fella Tchoosie, me catch'm. No good belonga you."

I was to drive the gently nurtured girl out of the house so that this foul creature might seize her as he would a struggling wallaby, and take her to live a degraded life in the camp! Explanations and threats were of no avail. Duckbill, who was unable to comprehend that he and others of the camp had by abandonment forfeited all rights to Soosie and that she was now a "white Mary," made it plain that he would forcibly abduct her if I would but give him the slight assistance of expulsion. Otherwise he would catch her himself.

Threatening the camp with the presence of the "big fella government" if he or any of them dared to interfere, I went off, while he shouted his orders to "hunt that fella close up karrie badgin!" (sunset).

Forthwith the house was put in a state of semi-siege. Soosie, with tearful eyes and tremulous hands, hysterically implored us to protect her from a fate worse than death. A message brought Dan, who first disdained to take Duckbill seriously. Told how Soosie had been wooed with gifts, and that her maternal uncle had officiously bestowed her upon the gaunt, ill-favoured king of the camp in accordance with tribal law, which regarded her as a mere chattel at the disposal of the whim and fancy of the nearest relative or at the demand of the most authoritative man, he became concerned and installed himself as Soosie's special guardian.

A few minutes after sundown Duckbill appeared, quite unconscious of offence against civilised customs, carrying a waddy with which to administer an anodyne should his capture prove the least refractory. Threats and scoldings were lost. He was incapable of comprehending why there should be a moment's hesitation about the fulfilment of his legitimate rights and demands.

Though protests were vain, the fact that Soosie did not show herself imparted some glimmering of sense of the situation to him, and he wandered off in the gloom grumbling "That fella too flash," and frankly announcing "B'mbi me catch'm."

For weeks Soosie kept within doors, or if she ventured out was accompanied by one or other well able and determined to protect her. Her nerves were at acute tension; her life that of a hunted creature; for though she thought her fate inevitable, she concentrated her mind on what seemed to others pitiably weak and inconsequent schemes for the bafflement of Duckbill.

Was it that some ineffaceable trait told her that the tribal law as expounded by Duckbill was so wise that resistance to it was vain, and that the trivial plans over which she worried were merely invented as a sort of temporary palliative? She scorned the possibility of existence in the camp, yet strove to contest it by the use of fantastical devices. She urged that Dan and I should get some fearsome masks and rush the camp in the gloom, at the same time setting off fireworks, and so create such terrifying effects that none would venture near the spot again. With bated breath, she even suggested that I should make a "death-bone" to be employed for the secret ill of Duckbill; she thus exposed the dross of hereditary superstition which rose to the surface during mental ebullition.

It was quite in the nature of things that under stress such a nature should break down. She nestled close to Dan, promising to be his sweetheart on the condition that, rather than that Duckbill should take her away, he would shoot her. If it came about that the dreadful black man was himself driven off or disposed of by some other means and the country made safe for her, then she would marry the man who had saved her, and she hoped that she might never disgrace him.

Dan accepted the guardianship. His hut was two miles away and on the far side of the river. He saw little of it for the next few weeks.

Duckbill and his friends, as we were well aware, knew of our plans for the defeat of his proposed outrage. If Soosie could be ceremoniously married to the faithful Dan, no black in the neighbourhood would endeavour to molest her. Indeed, all, even to Duckbill, would be flattered and demonstrative of pride in the alliance.

A fortnight later Duckbill again intercepted me. Since the previous verbal encounter I had gone armed. He carried, somewhat ostentatiously, a tomahawk and a couple of nulla-nullas.

"No good you keep'm that fella Tchoosie. Me bin look out plenty. That fella belonga me. Suppose you no lat'm come, more worse b'mbi. Me want mak'm that fella all asame black fella. You gib it Clare belonga Dan."

My fingers twitched on the butt of the revolver. It was an ultimatum. That which from other lips would have been resented as complacent insolence had to be endured with apparent calmness. Threatening him with all the consequences of a visit from the "big fella government," I hurriedly left, for I was not too sure of self-control.

A stricter watch than ever was maintained, for the least relaxation of precautions might have involved results for which a lifetime of regrets would not have atoned. Though of such a low type of the human race, the North Queensland aboriginal possesses certain admirable characteristics. His mind seldom swerves from a set purpose within view of attainment. He may be rebuffed and disappointed, and may assume indifference to or forgetfulness of his purpose; but in his heart he does not accept defeat until an absolutely decisive blow is received. Invisible to us, the old man persistently waited, and watched. The dogs frequently detected his presence, if their eloquent alarms and their excursions were to be credited. Though she continued to pit her wits against the secret cunningness of the dreaded old man, Soosie was often preoccupied, seeming to regard herself as one not primarily concerned. Her calmness was preternatural, contrasting strangely with her previous petulant agitation and tragic despair. She avoided Dan, while clinging with profuse demonstrations of affection to her foster-sisters.

The reason for her change of policy and manner was revealed with distressing suddenness. At daylight one morning the door of the room in which she slept under lock and key was wide open, and on her quaintly embellished table a primly written note:

"DEAR MUM,

"That horrible man who wants to take me away is right, and the Bible is right. I belong to this country, and must go. I would rather die than go to the camp; but I must know the big mountain. The dreadful people don't go there. They are frightened of it; I love it. I shall live there by myself till I die, and Dan will never be disgraced. You and Dada and Clare and Fan and

Bob have been all the world to me. You did your best to make me white at heart; but since this trouble began I have thought and thought, and found that the black in me smudges all the good out. Don't try to come after me. I shall hide. I would be too much ashamed ever to look at you again. Forget me, for I am nothing but an ungrateful little savage.

"SOOSIE"

In all haste Dan and I set out for the camp, a mile or so further in the jungle. It was situated in a natural, symmetrical clearing, a circus hemmed in by sullen vegetation, and upon which no plant save blady grass ever invaded.

The camp was deserted. Save for a few still warm spots indicative of artfully smothered fires, there were few signs to indicate recent occupation. An hour's search revealed definite tracks leading east—to the mountain.

No pains had been taken to baffle pursuers. Apparently the blacks had just wandered off aimlessly in obedience to a whim of the moment. There was nothing but conjecture to support the opinion that the decampment had anything to do with the disappearance of Soosie. Probably the blacks were aware, in advance of ourselves, that she had stolen away. If so, they would inevitably get her, having, possibly, the advantage of hours of start and being efficient in the art of tracking. Our plan was to hasten so that we might, if fortune favoured, be in time to save the distracted girl from the repulsive and obscene ceremonies to which she would be subject if she fell into the hands of Duckbill.

An hour's walk brought us to the foothills of the mountain. The tracks turned abruptly north, winding indeterminately as if no special object had been in view. It might be that while the men of the camp had been intent on following Soosie's tracks, the women and children had straggled after as if the quest was of no special concern to them.

In the broken country well in to the base of the mountain all traces of the exodus was lost, though bush instinct, supplemented by the actions of the dogs, gave sense of its direction. Blundering down into a ravine where blanched vegetation betokened complete seclusion from the sun, we clambered up the opposing steep emerging from an entanglement of jungle on a high and open ridge which commanded an unimpeded view to the west—a scene of theatrical clarity with a single theatrical smear. From a hollow far below slothful smoke filtered through the matted, sombre, dew-bespangled foliage, rose a few feet, and drifted abruptly, dissolving from diaphanous blue to nothingness. The resonant whooping of a swamp pheasant, antiphonal to a bell-voiced, crimson-crowned fruit pigeon in a giant fig-tree, the screeches of a sulphur-crested cockatoo as it tumbled in the air, evading the swoops of a grey goshawk, materialised the peace and the conflicts of a scene upon which no man had made mark.

The phantom trail of smoke betrayed the resting-place of the fugitives, though all tracks on the uneasy earth had failed. Odours of the jungle soothed my mind, contradicted the transaction of any unholy orgy, and gave assurance that the men had unravelled Soosie's wanderings until she had begun to ascend the mountain, and that, being then on strange and terrifying ground, they had abandoned the search, returning to familiar level country free from the excursions of dreaded spirits.

With light hearts we descended the ridge, and, plunging again into the dimness of the jungle, struck as direct a route as possible for the smoke-revealed camp. Crossing a narrow creek, we peered silently through the screen of ferns and banana plants, where in a secluded glade were the wanderers in happy festival.

Could any scene approach nearer the ideal? Men, women and children, mostly unclad, talking and laughing in modulated tones, while amusing themselves with trivial occupations and eating convenient food in the depths of the jungle, sanctified by distance and scene and sound! Peace smiled, propriety approved. They ate of the fruits of the earth. The fern-embowered stream gave them to drink. No sign of the white man, with his interfering and desolating ways, assailed the sight. It was as if the mist of centuries had lifted, and for once time-soiled mortals were permitted to gaze on a Garden of Eden free from danger and innocent of sin. There was none here to make the quiet folk afraid or discontented.

As I stepped out, the scene changed with pantomimic celerity. We were in the midst of a community of excitable and resentful people, who, viewing us, if not with active hostility, at least with surprise and anger, seemed embarrassed by guilty knowledge. None of the customary greetings welcomed us. None offered other than scowls.

"Where Soosie?" I demanded in authoritative tones of a boy accustomed to treat my slightest word with respect.

With averted face he sullenly said: "That fella Tchoosie he run away. He go l-o-n-g way, alonga mountain!"

"Look here! You no humbug. Where Soosie sit down? Plenty row along white man suppose Soosie no come back. That fella Soosie belonga Missis. Missis very sorry. She bin make'm Soosie all asame white Mary."

Still the face-averting boy reiterated: "That fella Soosie he bin go long way—more far. You fella make'm Soosie no good."

Others gathered round. Several carried weapons—nulla-nullas and wooden swords—and assumed hostile attitudes.

Dan became uncontrollably excited, storming for the production of Soosie, and being met with inconclusive statements and evasions. Being one who knew no fear, who deemed his questions justifiable, who felt himself more than a match for the whole camp, and was convinced that the blacks were in possession of essential information, he urged the policy of chastising the sullenness out of a couple of incommunicative boys. His attitude, and mine, hitherto, towards the blacks had been of cheery good-nature tempered with considerate authority. Present moroseness was novel, and he was eager to sweep it away with a sturdy stick, and thus to demonstrate that when a friendly white man visited a camp blacks should be deferential and alert to assist his mission.

In the mood of the men tragedy was inevitable unless both of us kept cool. What would be the ending of a fray between two white men and many armed blacks, some of whom were aching under a prolonged, however inconsequent, grievance against a white family?

"Look here, Dan. Leave those fellows alone," I said firmly but quietly. "There'll be sorrow for some if you begin a row."

"I don't care for a hundred blacks! I'd kick myself if I could not floor half a dozen single-handed! Where that Soosie?"

To distract attention from Dan, I moved off a few yards.

"What you ki-ki?" I asked of Wethera, who gnawed with concentrated satisfaction at a charred bone. "You ki-ki wallaby?"

"No wallaby! This one 'mandee' (hand) belonga Tchoosie!"

Scorched flesh and blackened bone had left their smear on the face of the kindest cannibal of them all. On the fire was a foot with charred ankle-bones; in a dilly-bag other fragments, but in Wethera's countenance no consciousness of evil-doing.

"Come here!" I shouted.

The excited man strode to the spot.

"Soosie," I said, in the calmest tones I could command, "has been murdered. This is a cannibal feast!"

With a bound he upset the gin, who shrieked as she grovelled in the embers.

"You wretches! You kill Soosie! I kill you!"

As he drew his revolver from his belt I seized his hand, and, restraining him as best I could for a moment, spoke authoritative and soothing words, and led him away weak and tremulous.

Not for many months—long after Dan had left the district—did exact information as to the fate of the hapless girl reach our ears. Wethera told of the tragedy. Duckbill had followed her tracks from the house towards the mountain, had overtaken her, and, since she had fought frenziedly, had "killed her alonga head little bit," not intending to kill her "dead, finis." Carried to the camp, it had been found out that she was actually dead. Then all had become stricken and run away.

By her obstinacy Soosie had offended tribal law. She had suffered. In the necessitous jungle animal food is never wasted, be it beast, bird, or reptile.

It had been an edifying sacrament, too, founded on immemorial truth, for had it not been devoutly believed that Soosie's most excellent and potent personality would remain with and glorify every participant?

BLUE SHIRT

"A strong, untutored intellect, eyesight, heart; a strong, wild Man."—CARLYLE.

Half a century ago, when hardy and adventurous men made laws unto themselves, and their somewhat hasty and inconsiderate hands began to sting the aboriginal population, there lived on this Isle a stalwart native whose force of character constituted him a captain among his fellows.

Possibly he was Tom's father. Before he passed away, Tom had often told that his father was king of this realm and a man of parts. He it was who harpooned a huge green turtle to the east. The game was so extraordinarily strong that others hastened to his aid, for the capture was beyond the capabilities of one man kneeling in a tucked-up sheet of bark. The whole fleet of canoes barely succeeded in towing the massive and reluctant creature to the nearest beach, and Tom was wont to tell that it took eight strong men to turn it on its back. It was "kummaoried" on the sand, and Tom oft pointed out the very spot as proof of the most famous feast within the range of tradition.

Let it be accepted, then, that Blue Shirt was Tom's father, since history is silent on the point, and none is left to question or authenticate it. He was a big man, and his son was like him. He was fond of colours; so, too, was his son. He was a fighter; his son's meritorious scars proved him worthy of his blood. He was a man in authority and full of territorial pride; his son's dominance was undoubted, for did he not chide the "big fella gubbermen" on its audacity in disposing of his Island—his country—even to a friendly white man?

Blue Shirt was the ruler and lawgiver of this Island when a barque strove with a cyclone which eventually shattered her to pieces and scattered her cargo of cedar-logs to the four winds. After the wreck a boat put out from a not distant port on a beach-combing cruise. The boat was known as the CAPTAIN COOK. About a hundred years before her namesake had reported that he had seen about thirty natives, all unclad, on an adjacent islet. With the captain was his mate, two other white men, a black boy, and a young gin. Many derelict logs were seen and certain wreckage, which made the boat's company inclined to the belief that some of the castaways might have landed on Dunk Island. They steered hither, anchoring in the evening.

Early the next morning three stalwart black boys put off in canoes to the CAPTAIN COOK, and, making friendly demonstrations, were invited on board. Food was given them, and to the leader the captain presented a blue shirt. No dweller of the Island had ever before possessed such a sumptuous and glorious garment. Indeed, if the absolute truth must be told, no dweller had dreamt of anything more desirable than an inadequate cloak laboriously wrought from the inner bark of a fig-tree, raiment sanctioned by the first of fashions.

Having made it known that they belonged to a neighbouring islet at the moment unfriendly to the overbearing Dunk Island tribe, Blue Shirt and his attendants mentioned that cedar-logs and other attractive flotsam bestrewed the beaches, and volunteered to conduct the strangers to the best places on the understanding that they, being alien and hostile, should remain under the protection of the rifle-carrying white men.

The captain, two men, and the black boy, followed Blue Shirt ashore; but, although he was conspicuously clad, could not find him or any other man. A few old and casual women represented the hospitable inhabitants, while Sabbath quietude brooded over the scene as they strolled along the yellow beach. By chance one of the party glanced towards the spot where they had landed, and saw half a dozen vigorous gins endeavouring to haul the boat above tideway.

How excellent the strategy!

The designing but faint-hearted women fled when the white men charged for the boat, which now was seen to be endowed with an incredible, uncanny rocking movement of its own. Looking beneath, they saw a huge cripple straining himself, Atlas-like, to heave it over. In spite of inferior legs, his brawny shoulders had almost accomplished the feat when he was unceremoniously interrupted. While he sprawled away, a mob of blacks rushed suddenly from the cover of some rocks, the leader of the assailants being Blue Shirt, who had painted his unclad parts martial red and white. The strength of the party was guessed at thirty. An exact census was not taken, for with spears and nulla-nullas and big swords, each warrior having the protection of a shield, the treacherous band swept on the deluded guests of their leader, whose hostile yells scandalised the meek phrases and friendly signs of a short hour before.

The captain, poor, outwitted man, had laid his rifle beside the boat. It was too late now to bring it into decisive action. Keeping close together, the defenders warded off the first rush with whatever came to hand. The rifle was recovered; but Blue Shirt, recognising that it represented victory, struggled for it determinedly. A spear was thrown at close quarters straight for the captain's neck, but one of the men deftly twitched it off, a feat that so enraged the warriors that they made him their special target, until at last one of their spears pierced his hand. Being rough and thready, the black palm-point made an ugly wound; but the resolute man drew it out, and, breaking the spear in twain, threw it into the boat, and as he did so, another grazed his abdomen. While he was thus defending himself against the spears and nulla-nullas of outrageous fortune, the captain made wide, sweeping movements with the butt of his rifle, and the other man and the boy, the boat being by this time afloat, tugged at the oars. The attacking party followed, the captain making good misuse of the rifle, the odd man and the boy occasionally perverting an oar to wrongful but, at the crisis, effective purpose, while the wounded suffered the hate of him who earns personal as well as racial animosity. He sustained a cut on the head from a wooden sword, yet he fought on, retaining his wits, while a kind Providence, and his own artfulness and agility protected him from hurtling spears.

The cost of the little excursion was paid in wounds and bruises and, eventually, putrefying sores, while the souls of all instantly mortified under the sight of triumphant Blue Shirt jeering and gesticulating as only an uncouth black dare, as he waved over his head a tomahawk he had abstracted from the boat during the morning's pleasant entertainment.

No one of the poor, depraved representatives of the race has any knowledge of the event in which Blue Shirt showed himself to be a successful plotter, a bold strategist, an original tactician, and a brave fighter. His son is dust. His grandson, though true in complexion, knows more about engines than he does of wooden swords and how to use them. The zest of life was with his ancestor, who during a long life had but one shirt.

THE FORGOTTEN DEAD

"Of lonely folk cut off unseen."

HOOD.

A few months ago chance bestowed the opportunity of listening to the conversation of one who for very many yearn has hung upon the skirts of civilisation. A bushman of rare resourcefulness, wide knowledge of the dry as well as the moist parts of North Queensland, a reader, and an acute and accurate observer of natural phenomena, he has often entertained me with the relation of episodes in his career which, though quite unsensational, is of the material of which the history of the bush must be compiled. He is now settled on a tidal creek, his nearest neighbours miles away. Independent of the regular assistance of blacks in the cultivation of his land, he is one of those who, while acknowledging no such thing as comradeship, and who, true to his sentiments, keeps them at arm's-length, has, albeit, acquired confidences rather unusual.

When his reading matter has become exhausted, he has sat night after night for months together absorbing the lore of the camp. To him has been disclosed many a well-guarded secret. Not unto every man who asks do the blacks tell their thoughts or impart their legends. You may study them; but they, too, are discreet students, who often keep their counsel while seeming to comply with your anxiety to learn of their ways and be wise as they are wise.

My friend is one of those undemonstrative, self-contained men in whom some of the coloured, cautious metaphysicians find a congenial soul. Therefore is he a compendium of much out-of-the-way and covert knowledge.

As we talked on the subject of the unexplained disappearances of men in the bush of Australia, he told the incidents of the forgotten dead to which these writings have special reference. I use my own words, so do not bind myself to historic exactness.

He had been away earning his own living, for his estate, fruitful as it is, did not then quite provide for his sustenance, markets being distant and far from consistent. Returning, he found the blacks who had associated themselves with his humble establishment had in the interval sought change of scene. The land that he called his had belonged to their ancestors centuries before Cook tied the ENDEAVOUR to that disputed and historic tree, and was theirs when he had first intruded. His hut, his horses, his implements, were much as he had left them. The camping-place of the blacks appeared to have been unoccupied for some time. Such was in accordance with usual happenings. Going about his lonesome work, he reflected that his dusky acquaintances would return in their own good time, and being a man of mental resource, the solitude was by no means irksome.

Within a fortnight they appeared unceremoniously, and, taking casual part in the ordinary work, the affairs of the isolated estate went on as smoothly as before. There was a stranger in the camp, a middle-aged man, timorous, and knowing little of the ways of white men. Of him scarcely any notice was taken. Yet in a few weeks it was evident that the stranger was determined to make himself pleasant. Accordingly, the white man refrained from advances, while for the love of mental exhilaration he pondered: "That boy wants to tell me something. He shall tell me all he wants to in his own way, while I will play the part of an indifferent auditor."

That the stranger had some secret on his soul was apparent. My friend resolved to receive that secret in the spirit of gracious condescension. So played he his part, and line upon line, here a little and there a little, the story was told.

Few of the tribe of the stranger had ever seen a white man. None had ever visited the coast. All were myalls, living naked among the mountains in gorges gloomy with jungle, and but rarely hunting on the foothills. One day consternation and curiosity spread through the camp. Three strange men with yellow faces and short black hair had been seen. They carried nothing in their hands, and seemed frightened. Thus the nervous couriers of the camp spoke.

Next morning the men took up the tracks, and, sneaking close up, followed, alert and unseen, the unsuspecting visitors to their country.

Bewildered in the jungle, the queer-looking men wandered aimlessly, moaning and wailing. They were lost. Suddenly the blacks appeared. Two of the strangers, glad of the company of any sort of human beings, smiled and gesticulated pleasantly, making it plain that they were hungry, tired, and frightened, and, longing to get back to the coast, would bestow upon their guides unheard-of blessings for safe-conduct thither. Strangely, the black men accepted the trust. Four each took a hand of the confiding strangers, and, pointing ahead and chattering, induced them to walk quickly in a direction in which by signs they indicated the dwelling of a white man.

The third wanderer had run away, blundering through the jungle, and the blacks had refrained from following him. Nodding gaily and jabbering volubly, but with mutual intelligibility, hosts and guests paced along a narrow track, each of the latter personally and firmly conducted by two of his newly found and most attentive friends. Others of the tribe, "like frightful fiends, did close beside them tread"; and while the escorts lured the yellow men with comforting pantomime, the frightful fiends fell on them suddenly with great wooden swords, killing them off-hand and on the very verge of the camp.

Willingly hurrying to the place of execution, the murdered men had saved the calculating blacks the trouble of carrying their carcasses.

Then four went back for the nervous escapee. He was safe, for the tracks were as obvious to them as a plough furrow to a European. Crouching beside a fallen, decaying tree, where bird's-nest ferns grew outrageously gross, they found him; and they jeered. He screamed and shouted in unknown tongue, while the brisk, stubby hair of his head stood on end. (My friend's hair-brush was alluded to in graphic illustration.) They struck him down, and, smashing in his head and seizing arms and legs, jogged back to the camp.

And the festival lasted many days, though plenty made gluttons of them all.

The forgotten dead were Javanese—deserters from a sugar-plantation; for the tragedy happened long ago, when labour was being drawn from Java and other oversupplied countries. Desertions were not uncommon, for the sanguine men of the equator endure with less philosophy than others that sickness of the heart which comes from love of one's native land when absent from it.

From Java's seething millions were the nostalgic three ever missed?

EAGLES-NEST FLOAT

"My raft was now strong enough to bear any reasonable weight."

ROBINSON CRUSOE.

Those who study primitive races, applying their wisdom and learning to the investigation of the origin of domestic and other implements and contrivances, inform us that the first boat was probably a log, on which the man sat astride, using a stick as a means of propulsion. In time the idea of hollowing the log occurred, Nature undoubtedly presenting the model and inviting the novice to squat inside. But what was the inhabitant of a certain island in the Gulf of Carpentaria to do since Nature failed to provide a tree big enough to possess the degree of buoyancy necessary for his frail frame, when he wished to cross the narrow channel separating him from a lesser island where turtle are plentiful and unsuspicious?

Being in status something above a wallaby—the largest animal other than himself of his native land which, when hunted, occasionally swam towards the opposite shore, he constructed one or other of two rafts or floats, both derivable from Nature's models. One was in the form of an eagle's nest, and not nearly so large as that in which some eaglets are reared, made by interlacing branchlets of white mangrove until the mass was sufficient to support his weight. With a double ended paddle rudely shaped from the thin buttress roots of the red mangrove, and comic in the crudeness and disproportion of its parts, he felt himself safe miles out to sea. When he approached a passing vessel he presented the illusion, not of walking, but of sitting on the water, for the float was almost completely submerged. If it became necessary for his wife to attend him on his marine excursions, she was towed behind, and used her own pedal power. Possibly this primitive raft is the pathetic expression of man's first struggle against the restrictions of the sea.

The other resource of the boatless islander was another description of float, also retrogressive from the log; the idea not transmitted to him by any high-minded bird, but forced upon his attention by elemental strife. He would have seen that the wind and the waves occasionally tore from his beaches Pandanus palms, and that the matted, fibrous roots thereof floated. Pondering in his dim way, and being sadly an hungered and aware that fat and lazy turtle were basking in the sighed-for shallows, he took a bundle of buoyant roots and light sticks and lashed it securely at one end with strips of bark. He then spread out the other end until it took the shape of a fan, and weaved the strands loosely together with beach trailers. His raft was complete. At least this description applies to that in use to-day, which represents the highest stage to which the design has been brought.

Under the influence of the peril-ignoring hunger, the hunter sat on the float with legs extended frontally. Across his thighs crouched his favourite dog, and behind him, her thin shanks outside his and her skinny arms round his slim waist, sat, uncomfortable, his cowed wife—a necessary part of his equipment. Can he be imagined half turning to his deferential spouse, and saying: "My dear, in the words of Shakespeare,

"On such a full sea are we now afloat
And we must take the current when it serves
Or lose our'—turtle"?

Is it not edifying, too, to reflect that the timid man, encouraged by the object-lessons of Nature, given in pity of his simplicity, had contrived the only rafts the resources of his island made possible? And does not the fact that he had courage to cross the estranging deep thereon give graphic proof of the inhospitality of his native soil?

Flat and generally of sad aspect, the country of the raftsman lies remote and uncommended. The scented sandalwood is there, dwarfed, attenuated, worthless. The most fragrant of the Pandanus palms is plentiful, the fruit forming the chief part of the vegetable diet of the lean and stunted inhabitants, who find difficulty in fashioning weapons with which to obtain fish and turtle, the land failing to supply straight sticks of the length needed for spears. Each has to be spliced. The islands are expressed in the race they sustain—possibly the lowest of Australian types. Does it not bespeak much to the credit of men and women who have been used to the cities where the advantages of civilisation are at command and its comforts available, that they should abandon the society of kin and friends and isolate themselves in a drear and unfriendly tract for the sake of a few coloured folk whose mental capacities are feeble and whose habits are shockingly disgusting?

NATURE IN RETALIATION

"Red in tooth and claw."

TENNYSON.

In a mangrove creek a shoal of barramundi had been bombed with dynamite. Immediately after the explosion the white onlookers as well as the blacks dived off-hand into the stream to secure the helpless fish. One of the party seized a weighty and unconscious victim of the outrage, and to retain it thrust his fist through the gills and found himself unable to withdraw, and when the fish began to revive he realised that he was not master. With a supreme effort he did manage to get his head above water to gulp a mouthful of air, but the gallant fish promptly exerted itself, and a deadly struggle took place on the muddy bottom. Once more the fish was tugged to the surface, only to dive just as the man became conscious of the applause of the interested spectators. When they came to the surface again ill luck on the part of the fish had brought it into the shallows caused by a ridge of rocks, and the man hauled his prize ashore, frankly acknowledging that the happy chance of the rocks and not his own wits and strength had given the victory into his hands.

On another occasion heartless dynamite was used in a creek, where had assembled many blacks, who scrambled riotously in the muddy water for the spoil, among which were several huge crabs, some dismembered by the force of the explosion, some stunned, some merely agitated. Dilly Boy, the biggest and the greediest of the crowd, acquired several fish and three or four crabs, the largest of the latter of which seemed sound asleep. The dynamite had ministered an anodyne from which, apparently, there would be no awakening. It the boy disregarded, while he secured those which were more or less active. Busily engaged, he was not aware that a crab when he seems asleep may be merely plotting. This hero was hatching out a scheme whereby it might be revenged for the outrage. It watched and deliberated, and as the boy sat down grabbed him with ponderous and toothed pinchers on that part of the body which is said to be most susceptible to insult. The boy rose. Not half a plug of dynamite could have given more hearty impulse, not all the clamour of a corroboree equal his yell of surprise and anguish. He capered. The crab, which had not speculated on the caper, and to avert summary divorce, locked its claws, now guaranteed to hold to death and beyond it—to destruction. Astounded—indeed, petrified—by the high antics of the boy, none of the spectators could venture to his aid. They were fully engaged with unrestrained and joyful hysteria. The more the boy yelled and cavorted, the more frantic the fun. Blood trickled down the chocolate-coloured skin, but the valiant crab held on. It was there for a definite purpose. The hour and the crab had arrived. Vengeance for centuries of wrongs to the race and heroic self-sacrifice animated brain and inspired the claw with the dynamics of ten; while the afflicted victim imagined—he had no mirror to hold up to Nature—that he was the sport of a lusty crocodile.

Amidst his shrieks he commanded the ministration of his wife. She ran to meet him with a waddy. True to the limitations of her sex, though her intentions were admirable and dutiful, the result was disastrous. The boy got a paralysing blow on the small of the back, and flopped down. Up jumped Dilly Boy, and the gin raced after him, murderously inclined to the crab. Half her blows were misses and the other half seriously embarrassed her husband, as his tumbles testified. She belaboured him impartially and with perverted goodwill from shoulder to heel, for she aimed invariably at the crab, and where is the woman who ever hit where she designed? The crab was merely tickling; the faithful spouse, with the tenderest motives, was cruelly beating her lord and master to disablement, and it can scarcely be credited that the echo of his remarks has yet subsided. In his fervour the boy made an exceptionally vicious threat against the gin, and in response she missed him and hit the crab. Under such forceful compulsion the crab parted with its claw. It was ponderous and toothed, be it remembered, and well and truly locked, and retained its grip. The target being smaller, the aims of the gin went more and more astray. The back of the boy, owing to the incessant misses of the waddy, changed from brown to purple, and a red ribbon wavered down his thigh. Still he ran, and the devoted gin coursed after him with the energy of a half-back, the fury of a disappointed politician, and the riot of three-dozen cockatoos scared from a corn-field. Almost worn out, the boy sprang round, and, seizing the waddy, began to chastise the gin, whose screams blended with his unwholesome threats. But the claws held on—not like grim death; they were grim death. Every second blow was directed aft—one blow forward, which generally severely disagreed with the gin; one blow astern, which afforded neither mental relief nor physical comfort. The gin fled from the infuriated boy; the boy from the fearsome relic of the crab, and called louder as he ran. When in full flight, the gin tripped over a mangrove root, and, spread-eagled, fell. The boy came tumbling after, but the remnants of the crab—the bony bud of a tail—stood erect and firm. Then the pitying spectators seized Dilly Boy, and, holding him, unlocked the pinchers. He rolled over—it was the only easeful attitude—as he cursed all gins, crabs, and dynamiters with wondrous fluency. And may the potency of those coloured curses rest upon the latter!

"STAR RUN ABOUT"

"It is the stars,
The stars above us, govern our conditions."

SHAKESPEARE.

Primitive folk have ever looked up to the heavens for signs of good and ill. Celestial appearances have fought for them terrestrial battles, or have weakened their arms by prognostications of impending disaster.

Appeals have been made to passionless planets for justice against mundane decrees, and when coincidences have been favourable the devout student of the skies has loudly proclaimed them as proof of supernatural interest in trivial, transient occurrences. In accordance with the degree of poetry in the fibre of the people, so, in a certain degree, has the belief in stellar influence been manifest.

The blacks of North Queensland, being, possibly, the least of the races in a poetic sense, have but slight regard for the interference of the stars in their poor little affairs, and in this respect are saner than many a nation which has given abundant proof of wisdom. One of their beliefs is that meteors are baleful, though under given conditions they derive from such phenomena longed-for assurance. A meteor is described as "Star run about." "That fella no good; him kill'em man!" Yet in circumstances to be mentioned they find in a meteor a sign that life has been restored to an individual whom they have done to death. It is the opinion of men who have studied the customs of the blacks that they—and to their honour be it said—were never among themselves premeditated, gluttonous cannibals. Human flesh was eaten, if not with solemnity, at least with ceremony, for the belief exists to this day that the moral and physical excellencies of the victim are assimilated by those who partake of his flesh.

Reincarnation is prompt and practical, and unaccompanied by wasteful and delusive hope. Herein lies the explanation of many a deliberate and confessed killing, while to the meteor have the perpetrators looked for absolution and remission of their sin. That which in the eyes of the white man is regarded as an atrocious murder has not been, in their semi-religious code, in any sense criminal, but a rite from which many if not all the camp must inevitably benefit.

In one respect the killing of a boy is the highest compliment which may be paid him, for it is proof that he has personal qualities which are the envy and admiration of others, and for general welfare should be shared by all. The boy who so dies is an unconscious patriot. This is proved sufficiently by the fact that only what are considered to be the more vitalising portions of the boy's body are eaten, whereas if gluttony were the impulse of the deed the whole of the body would be consumed.

An illustrative incident has been told me by one who has gained the confidence of the blacks, and to whom other facts connected with it were personally known. Not many years ago a boy from from a distant locality visited a certain district in company with his master. He was tall, well favoured, a good rider, quite an athlete, an accomplished performer with the mouth-organ and concertina; ready and persuasive of tongue. These qualities provoked unaffected admiration; for the natives of the place are undersized, ill-looking, and deficient generally in the arts of pleasing. Before the master left, Caesar was persuaded by his envious fellow-countrymen to remain with them to be flattered and courted.

To evade trouble, the whole camp took to the hills for a while. In the meantime Caesar's master departed, thinking, no doubt, that the boy would follow him to his own "more better country." After several weeks the local blacks returned, but Caesar was not of the party, and it did not occur to any of the white residents to ask questions concerning him. In accordance with the love of notoriety which affects humanity irrespective of complexion, one of the boys began to boast of being as good as Caesar, and to prove his contentions by aping the manners of his absent friend. It was not long before he blurted out the secret by which he had become superfine—he had participated with others in a cannibal rite after Caesar had been good-naturedly killed.

Rumours of the tragedy came to the ears of the police. The ringleaders of the assassins were arrested, and one at least endured a term of imprisonment as punishment. Caesar had been lured away and killed because he was a good fellow and strong, and because his murderers wanted to be good and strong like him. Certain parts of his body were eaten, without relish, but with fervent hope. A remarkable circumstance in connection with the sacrifice and ceremonial rite for the general welfare is that the perpetrators console and comfort themselves with the belief that should a meteor appear it is a sign that the victim did not actually die, or if he died under their hands, that he has come to life again. Those who were concerned in the killing and who had partaken of the flesh sat together for several evenings gazing with expectation into the sky. A meteor flashed across it, and it was hailed as a sign that Caesar was alive and had gone to his own country. The contrary evidence of relics of the dead was waved away before the imperious and disinterested testimony of the falling star. "No matter. That fella him no dead—finish. Him walk about 'nother country. Him good fella. That fella star run about bin tell 'em."

They felt themselves to have benefited materially and spiritually by participation in the rite, and were calm in their belief that the victim was none the worse for the temporary misfortune from which he suffered.

In another locality a meteor signifies the death of an individual, and is referred to as "Tee-go-binah." When a death cannot be directly attributed to it locally, the phenomenon is referred to with such rustic logic as this: "Some fella dead alonga 'nother camp. Might be longa way." The ancients felt "the sweet influences of the Pleiades." One of the two intimacies of the blacks of North Queensland with stellar phenomena which has come to my knowledge is associated with reincarnation after a deed of blood. Their faith is as absolute, perhaps, as was that of the men of old.

BLACKS AS FISHERMEN

"For I tell you, scholar, fishing is an art, or at least it is an art to catch fish." —IZAAK WALTON.

Along the coast of North Queensland evidence may still be obtained, though it ever becomes more difficult to secure practical demonstration, of several novel methods of killing fish in vogue among the blacks prior to the advent of civilisation. In many parts, indeed, the presence of the white man has swept away not only the use of decent, if trivial, pursuits and handicrafts, but the knowledge also that they ever existed.

The few facts here presented are, with some slight reservations, drawn from actual observation. No doubt the well-informed on such subjects will have plenary reasons—if ever these lines are honoured by perusal of the class—for the accusation that there is nothing in them having the virtue of newness or novelty. But I am not a professor with a mind like a warehouse, rich with the spoils of time, but a mere peddler, conscious of the janglings of an ill-sorted, ill-packed knapsack of unconsidered trifles.

Some pioneers know more about the acts of the past than the best informed of the younger blacks, who look with wonder and unconstrained doubt when shown articles similar to those which their grandfathers must have used almost every day.

Though the blacks of the past had but casual knowledge of the cruel little barb that the resourceful white fisherman finds essential to sport, and had neither neat tackle, nor reels, nor creels; though they were denied the solace of tobacco, and every other accessory, they were adepts at fishing. They had at command a stock of accumulated lore so graphically transmitted that the babe and suckling must have seemed to acquire it almost intuitively. They knew much of the habits of fish. Their methods of laying under tribute the harvest of the sea were so varied and unconventional that when one expedient failed, others, equally free from the ethics of sport, were available at the shortest notice. Fishing was not a pastime, but a serious occupation in which nearly everyone was proficient.

Times are changing; but still the mouths of smaller creeks are sometimes dammed, save for certain sluices and by-washes where puzzling pockets are set. Weirs formed by stakes driven into the sand and interwoven with twigs guide incoming fish into ingenious traps, whence they are scooped up in dilly-bags. Occasionally the whole camp, dogs and piccaninnies included, take part in a raid upon the sea. Men in deeper water, women and boys and girls forming wings at right angles to the beach, enclose a prescribed area in the ever shifting, mobile fence. Certain of the men have huge dilly-bags made of strips of lawyer-cane, and shaped like a ninepin with a funnel for a head. The tactics of the party combine to drive the fish towards the silent men having charge of the dilly-bags, who manipulate what certainly has the appearance of being a very awkward utensil in the water with great skill and alertness. Hurried to frenzy by the shouting and splashing of the crowd, and the flurrying of the surface with bushes, the fish dart hither and thither until most of them have found their way into the bags, at the only spots where, for the time being, peace and quietude prevail. At other times a somewhat similar design of basket is used for trapping eels.

Men armed with spears surround and exterminate a shoal detected in shallow water; and the boomerang and the nulla-nulla as well as the spear form the weapons of the solitary fisherman. On one of the islands of the Gulf of Carpentaria the boomerang (I am told) alone is used, the blacks being so expert that little is left to chance.

Though the wommera, or, as it is known locally, the yellamun, is common in the neighbourhood of Dunk Island, it is not employed as an accessory in the spearing of fish. Further north it is so almost universally, a combination of boomerang and wommera being the most popular form. This dual-purpose weapon is merely a boomerang to one of the ends of which is fitted a spur, which engages the socket in the butt of the spear. While on this subject, it is interesting to note that, though the common form of the implement for increasing the velocity and range of the spear is generally considered to be peculiar to Australia, its principle is embodied in a contrivance which was used for a similar purpose in the New Hebrides in Captain Cook's day.

Describing some of the arts of the inhabitants of Tanna, Cook ("Voyages of Captain Cook round the World," vol. i., chapter vi.) says that in the throwing of darts "they make use of the becket, that is, a piece of stiff plaited cord, about six inches long, with an eye in one end and a knot in the other. The eye is fixed on the forefinger of the right hand, and the other end is hitched round the dart where it is nearly on an equipoise. They hold the dart between the thumb and the remaining finger, which serve only to give direction, the velocity being communicated by the becket and forefinger. The former flies off from the dart the instant its velocity becomes greater than that of the hand, but it remains on the finger ready to be used again."

It is obvious that the Australian implement is much the more reliable and effective. Cook mentions that with the dart the Tanna Islanders "are sure of hitting a mark within the compass of the crown of a hat at a distance of eight or ten yards; but at double that distance it is chance if they hit a mark the size of a man's body, though they will throw the weapon sixty or seventy yards." Such a standard of marksmanship would be regarded with contempt by the average black of North Queensland. The use of this becket (introduced very many years ago by the Kanaka) is a fairly common accomplishment among coastal blacks.

In shallow water, too, fish are chased until they become so exhausted and nerve-shaken that they partially bury themselves in the sand, or endeavour to elude observation by concealing themselves beneath stone or coral, or by remaining passive among seaweed, trusting, no doubt, to protective tints and assimilation with their surroundings. Few of these stratagems of the fish are of avail when once a hungry black is on its track. The science of war, we are bidden to believe, is not designed for the slaughter of mankind, but so to impress the enemy with a demonstration of overwhelming power, force, and majesty, that he may become mentally unable or unwilling to offer resistance, because of its obvious futility. So it is with the black in pursuit of a fish or turtle in shallow water. By noise and bluster he works on the senses of the fish until it becomes semi-paralysed. Then he proceeds callously to the killing, which, in the case of fish, if his right hand is encumbered, he generally accomplishes by a crunching bite into the back-bone at the shoulders.

At rare intervals the black varies his tactics by a night attack, which is often highly demoralising. When the moon is on the other side of the world, with spears and flaring torches of paper-bark, he rushes in a band to raid the reef, to the dismay of startled and bewildered fish. Substitute for the gurgling cadences of semi-submerged coral and muteness and universal dimness instant noise and splashing, and dazzling lights here and there and everywhere, and it is not to be considered strange that the fish—tipsy with panic and confusion—fail to exercise their habitual alertness.

At a certain season of the year—November and December in the neighbourhood of Dunk Island—myriads of fish, about the size of a sardine, appear in shoals, an acre or so in area, or encircle the islands with a living, bluish-grey frill yards broad. The blacks bestow on this godsend, popularly known as "sprats"—HARENGULA STEREOLEPIS (Ogilby)—the name of "Oon-gnahr."

How skilfully does Nature dovetail her designs! This great multitude of fish appears when it is most needed. The terns (sea-swallows) are rearing their families, and ever need fresh food in unstinted quantities. The small fry come to an excited and enthusiastic market. Slim, silvery kingfish, grey sharks, and blue bonito, harry the shoals, ripping through them with steel-like flashes, and as the little fish ruffle the surface of sea or emerge therefrom in living silvery spray, in frantic efforts to escape, the terns take all they want, screaming with satisfaction. Then, too, the blacks join in the work of destruction. When the frill of fish lies limp on the beach, they fabricate a seine net, cheap, but admirably suited for the purpose. Long strands of beach trailers and grass and slender twigs are rolled and twisted up—apparently without the slightest art—into a huge loose cable eight inches in diameter. The men run out the cable into the water at right angles to the beach while still the gins, with nervous haste, are adding to its length. If it breaks, a few twists and pokes suffice to repair it. The men at the lead curve in towards the beach, and the gins and piccaninnies wade out in line to meet them. Gradually the cable, shocking in its frailty, is worked in, enclosing a patch of the fish in a perilous coffer dam. Tumult and commotion are almost as necessary contributories to the success of the stratagem as is the cable. But before they realise what has happened, they are in such close company that escape is impossible; dilly-bags are filled in a single dip, and it may take half an hour to pick out those "meshed" in the cable. It is all the work of a few minutes, and the haul often amounts in quantity to a surfeit for the whole camp.

One of these rude seines which was overhauled was composed largely of the long, leafless, twine-like branches of the leafless parasite CASSYTHA FILIFORMIS (which the blacks term "Bungoonno"), IPOMEA PESCAPRAE ("Koree"), Blady-grass ("Jin-dagi"), and the tough sprawling branches of BLAINVILLEA LATIFOLIA ("Gallan-jarrah"), the whole being reinforced with withes of CLERODENDRON IMERME ("Missim"), all of which plants grow on the verge of the sea.

Vast as is the congregation of small fry, it gradually fritters away, martyred to fish, flesh, and fowl. By the time the little terns are thrown upon their own resources the violet frill of the sweet islands is frayed and ragged, and drifts loosely in shabby remnants.

For large fish—groper, the giant perch, king, bonito, rhoombah, sweet-lips, parrot-fish, sea-mullet, and the sting-rays (brown and grey)—a harpoon and long line are used. When iron is not available a point is made of one of the black palms, the barb being strapped on with fibre, the binding being made impervious to water by a liberal coating of a pitch-like substance prepared from the resinous gum of the arral-tree (EVODIA ACCEDENS).

The point is eight or ten inches long, the barbless end being swathed in fibre so that it may fit easily into the socket of the eight or ten feet shaft. A long line is tied to a point above the swathing, and, being drawn taut along the shaft, is secured to the end by a series of clove-hitches. When the fish is struck the point is drawn from the socket, while the shaft acts as a cheek on, and an indicator of, its course when just below the surface. Such harpoons and lines are also used for the capture of dugong and turtle, the line being made of the inner bark (the bast layer) of one of the fig-trees, and is of two strands only. Occasionally the HIBISCUS TILLIACEUS is laid under tribute for ropes and lines, which, however, are not considered as durable as those from the fig. Nets, set and hand, are also made with twine from the fig or hibiscus.

When, at low spring tides, the coral reef is uncovered, small rock-cod, slim eels, parrot-fish, perch, soles, the lovely blue-spotted sting-ray, catfish, flathead, etc., are poked out unceremoniously with spears or sharp-pointed sticks from labyrinthine mazes, or from the concealment afforded by the flabby folds and fringes of the skeleton-less coral (ALCYONARIA), or from among the weeds and stones—a kind of additional sense leading the black to the discovery of fish in places that a white man would never dream of investigating. At this opportune time, too, huge, defiantly armed and brilliantly coloured crayfish are exposed to capture. A statement was published recently that this was the speediest of all marine animals. The assertion is much to be questioned, but there can be no doubt that the crayfish is a wonderful sprinter. Familiar with its lack of staying power, blacks race after it uproariously as it flees face to foe, all the graduated blades of its turbine apparatus beating under high pressure. Two or three rushes and the crayfish pauses, and then the agile black breaks its long, exquisitely sensitive and brittle antennae, deprived of which it becomes less capable of taking care of itself; or it may find its gorgeous armour-plates smashed with a stone or penetrated by a spear. For the most part, however, the crayfish lurks in coral caves, sweeping a considerable frontal radius with ever-shifting antennae—not in pride or conceit of their beautiful tints and wonderful mechanism, but with a pitiful apprehension of danger, for the admirers of the creature are many and ever so much in earnest—the earnestness of unceasing voracity.

Having a decided partiality for eels, the blacks of North Queensland have devised several means of capture, one of which does not call for the exercise of the least skill on the part of the individual whose longing for the dainty becomes imperative. His placid perseverance, too, is of no avail, unless luck favours. Wading in a shallow, mangrove-bordered creek, he blindly probes the bottom with a six-feet length of fencing wire, the modern substitute for the black palm spear. Frequently he trifles thus with coy Fortune for hours, an inch or so separating each prod; and again, in a spasm of indignant impatience, he stabs determinedly into the mud at random. Non-success does not make shipwreck of his faith in the existence of the much-desired food in the black mud, for as far back as his own experience and the camp's traditions go, substantial reason for that faith has been plentifully revealed. He returns to the monotonous occupation until an unlucky eel is impaled, and then it is given no chance of escape.

Pushing his spear a couple of feet through, the boy grips the prize with both hands, or bends the wire into the form of a hook. Fortune may continue to smile, and the boy takes several during the afternoon.

Many boys enhance the charms of solitude by ingeniously tricking eels, Nature presenting them with an efficient engine of deceit and destruction, so designed that neither the agitations of art nor the invention of science could much improve it. About two feet of the thong or lorum of one of the creeping palms (CALAMUS OBSTRUENS) is all that is necessary. These lora are armed with definitely spaced whorls of recurved hooks, keen as needles, true as steel, about one-eighth of an inch long. Three or four of the whorls are removed to provide an unfretful but firm grip. The pot-holes and shallow pools and gullies and trickling creeks are populated by nervous, yet inquisitive, semi-transparent prawns, upon which eels liberally diet. So silent and steady of movement is the boy that even the alert prawns are unaware of, or become accustomed to, his presence; and what is there to warn the eel, enjoying its comfort among the dead leaves in the gloomiest corner of the pool, of danger? Could any but a black boy detect the difference between the brown sodden leaves and the half-inch of body which the eel has unwittingly exposed? The "pig-gee" (as some term the lorum) is used with almost surgical delicacy of touch to hook away two or three of the leaves. Then it is placed parallel to whatever increased length has thus been made visible, and with a decisive twitch the eel is torn from its retreat and killed off-hand.

Even the shy, long-armed little prawns (PALAEMON AUSTRALIS) do not escape special means for their destruction. A pliant rod about four feet long is improvised from the midrib of the creeping palm before mentioned, to the end of which is fastened a slender thread of the same material, split off by using the nails of the thumb and second finger. This strand, which is about four inches long, is delicately noosed. Standing a few feet away from the water-hole, the black so manipulates the line that the noose encircles the tail of the prawn, which, making a retrogressive dart upon alarm, finds itself fatally snared. The prawns are not, as a rule, eaten, being reserved for bait.

In creeks and lagoons thin, hollow logs are submerged. Eels naturally seek such refuges, and in due course the boy dives, and, sealing the ends with his hands, brings log and eel to land. Dr. W. E. Roth mentions that crayfish and a certain fish resembling the rock-cod are similarly captured, and remarks that the log is lifted at an angle, with one hand closing the lower aperture, in which position it is brought to and held above the surface, when the water trickles out between the fingers of the sealing hand.

Yet another method (analogous to "bobbing") is practised for securing eels. Huge worms, found under decaying logs, are threaded by means of a needle formed of a thin strip of cane on a line from ten to twelve feet long until several feet of bait are available. The line is merely doubled, the ends made fast to a stout pole, and the loop dangled in the water. The boy fishes patiently, nor does he strike at the first nibble, but permits the eel to swallow slowly what might be considered an undue proportion of the bait, when it is landed and compelled to disgorge for the benefit of the next comer.

Among coastal blacks—all of whom may be said to be fishermen—some are ardent devotees to the sea. Others of the same camp restrict themselves to unsensational creeks and lagoons. The frog in the well knows nothing of the salt sea, and its aboriginal prototype contents himself with milder and generally less remunerative kind of sport than that in which his bolder cousins revel. Such a man, however, may possess aquatic lore of which the other is admittedly ignorant, and be apt in devices towards which the attitude of the salt-water man is adverse, if not contemptuous. The fresh-water man is skilful in the use of a net shaped something like the secondary wings of a certain species of moth, and expanding and closing similarly. It is made of fine twine (one-inch mesh), preferably from the bark of one of the fig-trees or the brown kurrajong, tightly stretched on two pieces of lawyer-cane each bent to form the half of an irregular ellipse. This net ("moorgaroo") is manipulated by two men working in concert, principally for the capture of eels. They do not wait for the eel to come to them, but by shrewd scrutiny discover its whereabouts under the bank of the creek or among the weeds and roots. Then one silent man holds the net widespread, or adroitly dodges it into intercepting positions, while the other beats the luckless fish in its direction with more or less fluster. The persistency with which the creeks are patrolled by men with spears, netted and poisoned, invites one to marvel that any fish escape, and yet once again quite a haul is made.

That great philosopher, Herbert Spencer, once in his life made a joke and confessed to it, with apologies for its littleness. Lunching at a tavern in the Isle of Wight, he asked: "Oh, is not this a very large chop for such a small island?" Similarly, I have been astonished at the apparent disproportion between the size of the eel and the insignificance of the creek whence the exultant black has hauled it.

An instance of the poor part which the slimmest eel plays when pitted against the Smartness and resourcefulness of the black may be related. A large eel, in a moment of indiscretion, showed itself in a fairly deep creek. Bewailing the absence of his wing-net, or "moorgaroo," the boy hunted the elusive fish hither and thither with cunning determination. At last it disappeared under a log. In most of his activities the black boy sniffs at conventions. Hastily stripping, the boy dived and when he reappeared the eel was vainly squirming in one of the legs of his trousers which had been knotted below the knee.

Another boy, a stranger, brought with him traditions which he successfully materialised in favour of the employment of several light darts instead of a single heavy spear for fishing. The subject was frequently debated, but none of the camp adopted George's theories. His favourite weapons were the dried stems of an all too common weed, which generally grows straight and true. Into the thick end he would insert a four-inch length of No. 10 fencing wire, sharpened to a delicate point, and with a battery of eight or ten of these he would sally forth. His bag averaged high. Often he treated me to practical demonstrations of the success of his methods. A big flathead reposed in two feet of water, half buried in the sand. George had one of his darts fast in a twinkling, and the fish flashed away, the tip indicating its movement. In a few minutes the hapless flathead was carrying no less than six darts, and as such a handicap was absurd it abandoned the race for life.

On another occasion he struck a big sting-ray so full of his impish darts that it resembled an animated pincushion of monstrous proportions. It, too, realised the futility of kicking against so many pricks. On the other hand, Tom, with his heavy shaft and barbed point, relied on a single weapon. It seldom failed, for his right arm was strong and disciplined to a nicety.

On a shallow tidal creek a settler had made a corduroy crossing of the fibrous trunks of the Pandanus palms, which the blacks of the neighbourhood turned to account in the capture of fish. A few frail sticks, artlessly interwoven with grass, formed a primitive weir at the down-stream end of the crossing. Fish which went up with the tide frequently found themselves stranded on the way down, for the water passed freely between the palm-tree trunks without affording them right of way, and the rude weir often stopped for ever belated bream, mullet, and barramundi. This simple trap, though it does not appear to be put into use on the coast generally, seems almost to indicate an instinctive knowledge of a studied design described to me by an observant friend who has travelled into many an odd nook and corner of Queensland. On a deep but narrow tributary of the Georgina River a permanent trap on a large scale was wont to be maintained. A tree had been felled across the stream so that each end of the trunk was supported by the respective bank. Straight stakes were driven firmly into the bed of the creek as closely together as possible, the heads resting against the horizontal tree-trunk. This palisading formed the base of an embankment of packed grass and rubbish, sufficiently tight to raise the level of the stream about three feet. In the middle of the embankment, and about one foot below water-level, a hole about one foot square had been cut. A platform about ten feet long by three feet wide, having a fall of about one foot and formed of a number of straight saplings laid parallel with the stream, and supported by a couple of transverse bearers on four stout forked sticks, received the escape from the sluice. At the lower end of the platform was a rough weir of twisted grass, which was continued up each side for about half its length. Water passed with little hindrance through the platform, while jew-fish, yellow-tail, and bream, were retained in considerable numbers.

Many years have elapsed—peradventure centuries—since the blacks of Missionary Bay, Hinchinbrook Island, built a weir of blocks and boulders of granite which oysters cemented here and there. On the fulness of spring tides fish frolicked over and among the boulders. Those which delayed their exit found themselves in an enclosed pool which at certain seasons of the year runs dry. To this day the sea continues to pay tribute, though the blacks of the locality have passed away, and there is none but the red-backed sea-eagle or the heavy-flighted osprey and a rare and casual white man, to receive it. Among the few emblems of the vanishing race, this persistent weir-taking toll of the fish month after month, year after Year, for the benefit of successive generations of eagles and ospreys, appeals vividly to the imagination.

HOOKS

From what can be ascertained at this late date, pearl shell hooks were very sure and killing, but seem to have been used principally for smaller fish—whiting, perch, bream, flathead, etc.—the occurrence of large hooks being exceedingly rare. Mullet (if tradition is to be credited) were seldom caught by hook and line, but were speared among the mangroves at high tide—a practice which prevails to this day. The Dunk Island examples have a resemblance to one of the forms of pearl-shell hooks used by the Tahitians in Captain Cook's day.

Tortoise-shell hooks capable of holding large kingfish and fair sized sharks are common among the natives of Darnley Island, Torres Straits. During the process of cutting and paring the hooks to the size and design required, the shell is frequently immersed in boiling water, which temporarily overcomes its inherent toughness. Incidentally, it may be pointed out that the evidence derivable from these fish-hooks does not afford proof of Papuan influence on the mind of the Australian aboriginal, except at the extreme north of Cape York Peninsula and a few miles down the eastern coast of the Gulf of Carpentaria. This default seems the more remarkable in face of the fact that outrigger canoes, doubtless of Papuan or Malayan origin, were known as far south as the Johnstone River.

To say that the coastal blacks of North Queensland had no knowledge of the use of barbed hooks is misleading. In sheer desperation, when the supply of pearl-shell hooks was exhausted, they were wont to attach bait to their harpoon-points, and they used such unpropitious means successfully, and occasionally made a miniature hook by tying a sharp spur to a thin, straight stick. Recent proof has been obtained of the use of the lorum of one of the creeping palms, from which all the spurs save three at the thicker end were scraped off. With the knowledge of the efficacy of the barb under extraordinary circumstances, is it not the more remarkable that they failed to employ it systematically? Dr. W. E. Roth describes crescentic hooks of coconut shell and wooden hooks with bone barb, and also barbs improvised from one of the spines of the catfish. He also mentions as "the most primitive form of hook" the dried tendril of HUGONIA JENKENSII ("pattel-pattel" of the Dunk Island blacks). To anyone familiar with the crescent pearl-shell hooks, the use of the singular tendrils of the Hugonia would immediately be suggested; but my observation, inquiries, and opinion do not support the theory. The shape of the tendril is all that can be said in its favour. It is neither sharp nor tough enough for actual use.

With these barbless hooks the bait was not impaled, but strapped on with shreds of bark.

NARCOTICS AND POISONS

It is said of the great Mogul Emperor Babur that he boasted of being able to make fish drunk so that he might haul them in shoals, and when "Carathis" pronounced her "barbarous incantations" the fish with one accord thrust forth their heads from the water. Is it generally known that the North Queensland blacks also are expert in the use of narcotics and indifferent to the ethics of sport? The most commonly used of the fish poisons on the coast of North Queensland is likewise employed by the natives of Zambesi Land for a similar purpose. The plant is known botanically as

"Derris." Two varieties, "scandens" and "uligijiosa," are known in this State. The aboriginal titles vary in different localities, but "Paggarra" will suit the present purpose. Some blacks are so offensively civilised that they know the plant by the name of "Wild Dynamite." Possibly it owes its popularity among fish poisons to the fact that it is the handiest of all. It trails over the rocks, just out of touch of high-water mark, but not beyond the reach of the spray of surges. With roots investigating inclement crevices, and salt air damping its leaves, the plant flourishes, and flowers prettily in graceful racemes. In the semi-obscurity of the crevices the flowers put on a tinge of pink, literally blushing unseen. The heartless blacks tear up the plant, branches, leaves, flowers and all, coarsely bundle them together, and, wading into an enclosed pool where fish are observed, beat the mass (after dipping it into the water and while held in the left hand) with a nulla-nulla. The action is repeated until the bark and leaves are macerated, and then the bundle is thrown into the pool. In a few minutes the fish rise to the surface, gasping and making extraordinary efforts to get out of the infected water. Death ensues rapidly, but the fish are quite wholesome as food.

Another of the vegetable poisons is known as "Raroo" (CAREYA AUSTRALIS). The bark at the base of the trunk and of the roots contains an effective principle, which is released in a somewhat similar fashion to that employed with "Paggarra."

The fruit of the handsome, shrubby tree known botanically as DIOSPYROS HEBECARPA is also a most effective fish poison. It is oval-shaped, red when ripe, and, as the name implies, covered with soft, fine hair. For all its lofty title and attractive appearance, the fruit is deceptive, for it bites and blisters the lips and tongue like caustic, and on being bruised and thrown into a pool on the reef, all fish are killed outright.

A different and, for a black, singularly complicated process is employed for the extraction of the noxious principle residing in the plant known as "Koie-yan" (FARADAYA SPLENDIDA). This is one of the most rampant and ambitious of the many vines of the jungle.

It combines exceeding vigour with rare gracefulness. The leaves are a light glossy green, ovate, and often a foot long, while the flowers are pure white (resembling slightly the azalea, but free from its fragility), large, and with an elusive scent, sweet and yet indefinite. The fruit, smooth and of porcelain whiteness, varies in size and shape, and is said to be edible, though blacks ignore it. A large marble and an undersized hen's egg may dangle together, or in company with others, from the topmost branches of some tall tree, which has acted as host to the clinging vine. The handsome but inconsiderate plant is turned from its purpose of lending fictitious and fugitive charms to quite commonplace but passive trees to the office of stupefying uncomplaining fish. But the element which holds such deadly enmity to the sense of the fish is not obtainable by the simple primary means successful with other plants. Indeed, the process is quite elaborate, and goes to prove that the Australian aboriginal has to his credit as a chemist the results of successful original research, and that he is also a herbalist from whom it is no condescension to learn. In this detail, at any rate, he is distinctly an accomplished person. Portions of the vine are cut into foot lengths; the outer layer of bark is removed and rejected, the middle layer alone being preserved. This is carefully scraped off and made up into shapely little piles on fresh green leaves. One might imagine that a black boy preparing the deadly "Koie-yan" was really playing at chemist's shop with neat-handed scrupulousness. When a sufficiency is obtained it is rubbed on to stones previously heated by fire. The stones then being thrown into a creek or a little lagoon left by the receding tide, the poison becomes disseminated, with fatal effect to all fish and other marine animals.

It is pointed out, however, by Dr. Hamlyn-Harris that the nature of the active principle of the "Koie yan" does not permit of elaboration by such means. The heating of the shredded bark would, therefore, appear to fall into line with the gibberish of ancient alchemists. It would bewilder the uninitiated without enhancing results.

Many other plants supply the means of killing small fish wholesale, or of reducing them to palsied cripples. The three described are fairly common, and have, therefore, been selected to point a moral. Poisoning fish is a poor sort of sport, perhaps, but there are two classes of fishermen—the hungry and the artistic. The latter use flimsy tackle and complicated gear, and play the game, giving the victims to their wiles a sporting chance. Though not the only representative of the hungry class, the black boy generally fishes on an empty stomach, and his demeanour coincides. No slobbering sentiment affects him. Yet he is not so cruel as the mean white who throws a plug of dynamite into the river while the fish are enjoying their crowded hour, though he will with as little taint upon his conscience poison a pool full of fish as drag with hooked stick a reluctant crab piecemeal from its burrow among the mangrove roots. But then he is responding to the appeals of a clamant and not over-particular stomach, while your dynamitard is occasionally a well-fed barbarian with a queasy palate.

FLY-FISHING

The neatest and most artistic method by which the blacks kill fish necessitates the employment of a particular species of spider known to the learned as NEPHILA MACULATA PISCATORUM. This spider was discovered on Dunk Island by Macgillivray, the naturalist of the expedition of H.M.S. RATTLESNAKE in 1848. It has a large ovate abdomen of olive-green bespangled with golden dust; black thorax, with coral-red mandibles; and long, slender legs, glossy black, and tricked out at the joints with golden touches. A fine creature, gentle and stately in demeanour, it spins a large web, strong enough to hold the biggest of beetles and other insects, and, to harmonise with the superior air of the manufacturer, the gossamer is of golden-green. The great spider at the focus of the resplendent web is a frequent and conspicuous ornament to the edges of the jungle, and having no fear, and no indocility of temper, it undergoes the ordeal of admiration with an assumption of disdainful coquettism. The local name of this comely creature is "Karan-jamara." Shameless polyandrist, she maintains several consorts—from three to five seems to be the average number—and they, semi-transparent, feeble, meek, subdued little fellows, maintain precarious isolated existences in the outskirts of the web.

Though my own experience is negative, direct incontrovertible evidence is extant to the effect that birds often meet their fate by blundering into the web, to be devoured by the nimble and gaily decorated owner. I have frequently seen karan-jamara disposing of hard-shelled beetles as big in bulk as some birds, and the strongest of butterflies, once entangled, is powerless. The long-legged spider leaps on the struggling prey and stills its beating wings with one pinch of powerful red mandibles. March flies form the most frequent diet. One has been observed to dispose of fourteen of the great stupid flies in a single evening, and if the flies could reason they might, while whimpering because of the existence of such voracious spiders, acknowledge that they design their webs in a very perplexing and masterly manner.

In pursuance of inquiries—the results of which are herein recorded—a casual black boy, a stranger to these parts, and therefore unfamiliar with the local name and the special purpose to which the spider is put, was cross-examined. At first he failed to recognise the photograph, but when it was explained by the pointed allusion to a living Maltese-cross spider close at hand, a gleam of intelligence brightened his bewildered face, and he delivered a self-satisfied dissertation on the order Arachnida that is worth quoting:

"That fella Oo-boo-boo. That fella mammy belonga 'nother fella altogether. You no savee, come close up—that fella ply way. You no savee, come close up, that fella no good; that fella vite."

And the boy looked gravely sagacious and smiled the wide, wise smile betokening proud superiority of information. Had Macgillivray but known that the "Oo-boo-boo" was the parent of all the many species, and that it belongs to the discreetly valorous class that "vites" and flies away, and lives to "vite" another day, he might have achieved renown of a more popular kind than is the reward of the unromantic naturalist who discovers merely a superior spider.

This spider is used on some of the rivers as a lure, virtues almost irresistible being ascribed to it. Experiments in salt water, though not absolutely negative in their results, have not afforded any specially exciting sport; but possibly the fascination of the lure is more efficient in fresh than in salt water, and is influential over the habitual caution throughout a certain species of fish only. The trick is worked in the following manner:

The angler takes a light, thin switch and entangles one end in the web, which, by dexterous waving action, is converted (without being touched with the fingers) into a strand about two feet long. The spider is secured and squashed, and the end of the line moistened in the juices of the body, some of the fragments of which are reserved for bait, and also to be thrown into the water as a preliminary charm. These buoyant titbits attract shoals of small fish, among which the line, with its extract of spider, is delicately trailed; a fish rises to the lure, the gossamer becomes entangled in its teeth, and it is landed by a brisk yet easy movement of the wrist. A great angler recently said that throwing a fly is an act of feeling or instinct rather than reason. So the black boy with a careless flourish fills his dilly-bag, while he smiles at the serious attempts of the white man to imitate his skill.

Owing to the brevity and the frailness of the line, the catch is limited to fish under the recognised standard as to size. Tests prove that the breaking strain of the line is nearly three-quarters of a pound, but the weight of the individual is of no great consideration, since numbers are caught quickly. The gossamer is singularly sticky. The viscid substance with which it is coated is not readily dissolvable in water; indeed, water seems to have the effect of hardening it, so that the line' wears longer than might be expected. Piquant morsels of the spider are entangled in the frayed end of the line as its original potency becomes non-effective.

A friend for whose edification this novel method was demonstrated thus writes it:

"It did not take the boy long to get ready. They simply broke a switch about three feet long and attached a portion of the web about six inches long to the end; squeezed out on to a leaf the fluid internals of the spider, into which they dipped the end of the line, started a rather melodious chant, and put the line in shallow water. I was only a few feet away and could see no fish at first, but they came very soon. They were very small, about one and a half inches long. They fasten their teeth in the web, and are lifted out quite slowly. Some require to be pulled off the line after being landed. I watched for about ten minutes, during which time seventeen were caught."

Sir William Macgreggor, ex-Governor of Queensland, has described the Papuan art of fishing by means of kites, the lure being a tassel of the web of a spider of the Nephila species. No doubt the blacks here made an independent and original discovery, and in their simplicity applied it in a different, but none the less effective, style from that of the advanced Papuan.

Thus, to use the web and the fragments of a spider for fly-fishing is certainly meting out poetic justice to the spider on account of the many ensnared flies; and the black angler never pauses to reflect whether the comminuted remains of a spider can possibly be construed into a fair fly.